728(5)

QUINEY

HOUSE
AND
Home

Southampto
Institute of Higher Edu

HOUSE

AND

Home

A HISTORY OF THE SMALL ENGLISH HOUSE

ANTHONY QUINEY

BRITISH BROADCASTING CORPORATION

For my mother, father and brother
As a reminder of our home at '236'

This book accompanies the BBC Television series *House and Home*, first broadcast on BBC2 from Spring 1986

The series was produced by Suzanne Davies

Published to accompany a series of programmes prepared in consultation with the BBC Continuing Education Advisory Council

Line illustrations: Oxford Illustrators Ltd

This book is set in 10/12 pt Plantin
Typeset and printed by Jolly & Barber Ltd, Rugby, Warwickshire

© The Author 1986
First published 1986
Published by the British Broadcasting Corporation
35 Marylebone High Street, London W1M 4AA

ISBN 0 563 21133 4

Preface

This book owes its origin to the BBC Television series, also entitled *House and Home*, which was produced by Suzanne Davies. When I was approached for advice on this project, I was immediately attracted to it. For some years I had given a course of lectures to the School of Architecture and Landscape at Thames Polytechnic on the theme of houses and housing, starting with the medieval peasantry and ending with modern urban families, so this was a wonderful opportunity to contribute to the series and to address a wider audience than architectural students.

Although there are already numerous books about the smaller English house and the history of its architecture, it was agreed that the emphasis in this one should be as much on the people who lived in these houses as with the houses themselves. We wanted to concern ourselves not so much with architecture as with how architecture fits into the history of the people who built them and lived in them.

To write such a book was a daunting prospect. A complete history in this form would need a very long book indeed, and that was out of the question. I therefore decided to write eight short, but linked essays related to the individual television programmes. These are based on the research I carried out for my lectures at Thames Polytechnic, and for another book I am in the course of writing on the architectural history of the English farm. To add to this I had the benefit of Suzanne Davies's own challenging views on the subject, and the help of numerous friends and colleagues. To all of them I owe a great debt of gratitude.

I also want to thank the very large number of householders who have willingly let me tramp my way through their homes and who have discussed them with me. These people are far too many to mention by name, but every one of them has helped, whether or not their houses are mentioned here or included in the television series. I must add that nearly all the houses I have included in the text are private homes and not open to the public. Then I want to thank the archivists, librarians and keepers of the Greater London Record Office, the Society of Antiquaries of London, Thames Polytechnic and numerous local collections and museums for answering all kinds of questions and producing relevant documents and other source material with such rapidity. Here I should say that those books that are of specific relevance to the text are included in the Booklist, but an extremely large number of other books, articles and all unpublished sources on this wide subject have had to be omitted for the sake of brevity.

I cannot end without mentioning some of the people who gave me specific information on a variety of points or who helped in all kinds of ways with the text. Here I owe a great debt to John Smith who put the material for his forthcoming book on Saddleworth houses at my disposal, and to Nigel Morgan who took me on a whirlwind tour of the nineteenth-century housing of north Lancashire. Similarly I am grateful to the members of Co-operative Development Services, Merseyside Improved Houses, the Hesketh Street, Leta-Claudia, Prince Albert Gardens, Thirlmere, and Weller Streets Housing Co-operatives for my memorable introduction to their great experiment. Then I would like to thank my friends in the Historic Buildings Division of the Greater London Council, and Malcolm Airs, Jennie Allen, Susan Beattie, Di Bligh, Mary Cosh, Ginnie Hole, Alison Kelly, Frank Kelsall, Alan MacDonald, Bob Machin, Fiona Mackenzie, Judy Moore, Linda Newsham, Anne Partridge, Marion Quiney, Paul Slane, Nicholas Taylor, Robert Thorne and Michael Wadhams.

Finally, a subject such as this is bound to be controversial. This book is too short to do more than note some of the unresolved issues. Even a concisely argued opinion on some of them was out of the question. Nevertheless the book does represent my own views, even to the point of occasionally parting company with the television series. If it stimulates argument, that is all to the good; at all events I hope it stimulates a fresh interest in a subject that we all know a little about from personal experience, but which, when you look into it more closely, is actually endless.

Anthony Quiney
August 1985

Contents

Map of Locations

This map shows the places mentioned in the text; below are listed the types of houses found there and the chapters where they are described.

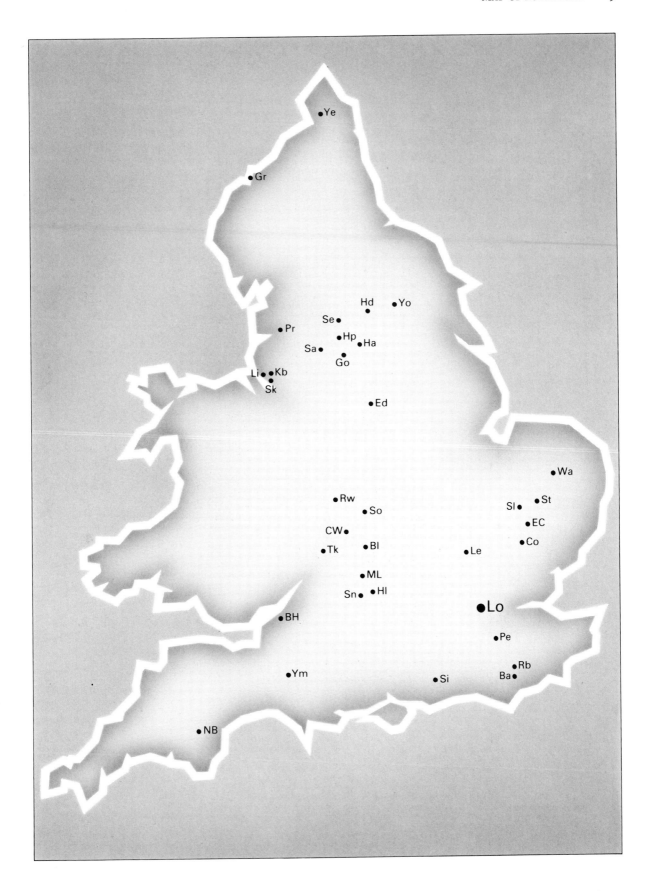

CHAPTER ONE
The Yeoman's Hall

Other people's homes are fascinating. Every year we pay a fortune and tramp mile upon mile round the nation's country houses, all to see how the aristocracy and the landed gentry lived. In a curious way we are proud of these stately homes. Some of them, after all, are great monuments of architecture. But that is not exactly what matters. We go because they are part of our heritage. Similarly, we travel miles to see a pretty village. Those happy groups of parish church, inn and old houses set round a green are again part of our heritage, and we are proud of them too. Besides, these are the places where we imagine our distant ancestors lived.

Those villages, or rather their images, are everywhere – on postcards, calendars, chocolate boxes and posters. The image seems to be more dear to us than the reality. Perhaps that is because we know so little about the ordinary people who lived in those places, certainly when compared with the public lives of the people who lived in our stately homes.

What, then, went on behind those pretty façades, looking on to the village green? You can start to find out if you actually do look behind them. You must look round the sides of the houses. You must see the back as well as the front, the inside as well as the outside. You must learn to understand the evidence that they have to offer. When you have learned to look at a house in a way that will let you understand how it was once used, it will no longer seem humdrum, however commonplace it may be. You will see it as a home, and moreover as a home that has sheltered generation after generation, rich and poor, from when it was built until the present. If only they could tell, people say. Houses can tell, if you know what to look for.

The Essex village of Earls Colne has something to tell, like every other village, though it does not belong to the world of the chocolate box in the way that, say, the nearby Finchingfield does. The church,

High Street, Earls Colne, showing some of the shops, including the Co-op supermarket at Nos 37 and 39, that obscure sixteenth-century timber-framed houses.

the inns, the houses and the greens are all pretty, but they never quite come together to form one of those timeless views that we believe are the essence of our heritage. Yet even a cursory look at the High Street shows that the village is fairly ancient.

A number of houses have old timbers on their fronts. This is not the decorative timbering we see on many Victorian and Edwardian suburban houses, but a genuine part of a structural frame. Timber framing was widely used for houses between 1200 and 1700. This immense period between the reigns of King John and Queen Anne changed England from a medieval feudal society to a parliamentary state on the verge of making those inventions that started the Industrial Revolution. It also changed the way people lived.

The timber houses of Earls Colne belong to this period. When we look at the sides of these houses, and the backs and especially the insides, more and more old timbers come to light. This is to be expected of houses of this period. Even so, the appearance of part of a timber frame inside one particular building is utterly astonishing. Nos 37 and 39 High Street are today a supermarket, filled with row upon row of tins and packets and jars. Nothing could be more ordinary. But look up! Suddenly there is a break in the modern ceiling to expose high above you a timber frame. It was once part of a house built at the end of the Middle Ages, probably about 1500. Later it was a farm, and what we can still see was the framing of an upper room and the roof of the farmhouse. Until 1571 it was owned by the Mallory family, and they gave the farm its name, 'Mallories'.

We know this because a number of documents survive that relate to Earls Colne. They help us to understand its buildings. Both the buildings and the documents have given Michael Wadhams and the Earls Colne branch of the Workers' Educational Association, led by Christopher Johnson, the basic material for a study of the village. It shows why the village has its present appearance, and provides an insight into the lives of some of the people who made it. This lets us see buildings both as structures and as places where people lived and worked. Architectural history and social and economic history come together in this study. Political history also has a role, because much of the village was owned by the de Veres, earls of Oxford, and as lords of the manor they governed Earls Colne. It was their land, and their permission to build had to be obtained at the manor court, and a small fee or fine paid at the same time.

Many of the villagers were their tenants and held land by agreement. A copy of this agreement appeared in the manor's records. For this reason a tenant came to be known as a copyholder. The records were kept on long rolls of vellum known as manorial rolls or court rolls because a meeting of the manorial officials and its tenants was known as a court. These court rolls tell us a lot about how the village came to be built, and how the villagers lived.

Architectural history is usually about monumental buildings, the stately homes of the aristocracy, the manor houses of people like the de Veres and churches like the one at Earls Colne that they helped to build. But architectural history is also about what is called 'vernacular architecture'. All the shops, inns, houses and farms at Earls Colne – indeed, all the homes and workplaces of the common people – are

Earls Colne: the Co-op supermarket at Nos 37 and 39 High Street, where the upper storey of a former timber-framed house is suspended over the shelves of food.

examples of vernacular architecture. The term applies to traditional buildings with traditional forms, built in traditional ways with traditional materials and using traditional decoration, buildings where every part is handmade. Vernacular buildings such as houses come in many different types. Any one type of house is likely to be very common in one particular district but not necessarily elsewhere. House types were subject to change, one evolving from another and often quite quickly, but it could be some time before they were accepted.

Some writers have thought of vernacular architecture and the architecture of the aristrocracy as separate, and even with separate origins. The rulers did one thing, the 'folk' another. That is not borne out by the facts. Architectural features, however grandly they start, tend to descend in society over the years, and are eventually taken up by the common people, who rarely started fashions of their own.

Vernacular and aristocratic architecture. Two late medieval houses in Warwickshire.
Left: a cruck-framed hall-house at Stoneleigh, built by a fairly poor peasant.
Below: Compton Wynyates, a grand house with a hall of the 1480s enlarged by Sir William Compton.

Whatever kind of building you are studying, the fundamental questions to ask are who built it and when. It is not enough to answer 'who' with a single name. No one builds in isolation. Owners and occupiers, architects and developers, craftsmen and labourers could all be involved, and any one of them might claim the major role and call himself – or herself – the builder.

These questions of who were the builders and when did they build are often hard to answer because the documents are missing or unclear. Even in Earls Colne, where there are many documents, the answers are only fragmentary, but they have a general application. What you discover about one house can be applied to other, similar houses. Historians can then take the evidence of a multitude of houses together and answer questions beyond the fundamental who and when. They can start looking for answers to that most important question of all, why.

Returning to the buildings in Earls Colne, then, we see more than timber frames among the additions of later centuries. We see the remains of old houses and workshops that illuminate the social and economic conditions of the past, and the ties between the landowners, the aristocratic de Veres and the village tradesmen. Nos 112–114 High Street, for example, are obviously old. Their age shows because the timber framing of the upper floor is still visible on the outside. Going inside you find a timber roof structure of the type used in Essex until about 1550. This house was probably built a few decades beforehand. From the court rolls we know a few of the copyholders who occupied this plot of land, both before and after the present house was built. At the beginning of the fifteenth century there was a large building here occupied by William Sonningwell. His widow Christina was a baker and brewer, and from 1425 she occupied a room next to what was described in the rolls as a 'hale spence'. This was probably a room for

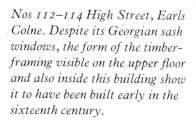

Nos 112–114 High Street, Earls Colne. Despite its Georgian sash windows, the form of the timber-framing visible on the upper floor and also inside this building show it to have been built early in the sixteenth century.

Nos 112–114 High Street, Earls Colne.
Left: The timber frame of the upper floor projects beyond the ground floor by about 2 feet. This projection is called a jetty and is produced by extending the floor joists outwards.
Above: The front of the jetty carries a fascia-board. These are usually decorated with carving or moulding. This one has a frieze of oak leaves punctuated by stars, the device of the de Veres, lords of the manor.

storing and selling ale (hale), and essential to her trade. In 1526 the site was acquired by John Pennock, whose family were in cloth weaving. He may have provided the money to build the house we see today. These scraps of information do not reveal to us how the house came into existence. Even so, it is interesting to know that brewing and perhaps the selling of ale were undertaken here. It is doubly interesting to have confirmation of women working as brewers, and to see an individual woman apparently leading an economically independent life at the end of the Middle Ages, a time when men dominated society. It is hardly surprising that the new house may have been built from the profits of weaving. After agriculture, weaving was one of the greatest sources of wealth in the sixteenth century in this part of Essex.

There is further evidence of weaving as a source of wealth a short way up the road. No. 15 High Street is now a small supermarket, a modern use in what seems to be a relatively modern building. But that is only a superficial view. A close investigation reveals that much timber framing of an old building survives inside. The building is in two parts, the front including the shop and the rooms over it, and a projecting range at the back apparently added later. The court rolls suggest that the front was built at some time before 1450 and occupied in 1441 by William Boon, a blacksmith. His was a necessary craft in every village for manufacturing and repairing ironwork from agricultural equipment like ploughshares to household goods like the pots you would hang over your fire. The upper room in the projecting range at the back has so much exposed framing visible inside that it appears at first sight to be a modern replica. In fact it is at least four hundred years old and seems to have been a loomshop. The evidence for this comes from the remains of long bands of windows of the kind provided in other loomshops so that weavers could see to work. The court rolls confirm this. In 1566 Robert Ennowes, a weaver from Coggeshall, acquired the premises by marriage. He would be just the person to have built the loomshop. So this High Street sets beside the land-owners, the aristocratic de Veres, the ordinary village people, Christina Sonningwell, John Pennock, William Boon and Robert Ennowes.

There is, of course, much more that we would like to find out, not just about these houses in Earls Colne, but about others around England more generally, and again not just towards the end of the Middle Ages but from as far back as we can go and right up to the present. To start with, why were these houses built in the form that they had? Did the occupiers choose, or did the landowners? If the villagers chose, did they try to emulate the landowners in what they built, for reasons of fashion or status, or were they prompted rather by the requirements of their particular usage? Who paid for their buildings, and where did the money come from? Did comfort and privacy mean anything to these villagers as they do to us today? Did the building craftsmen decide what was built because they could only provide a small range of build-ings? Tradition was a strong factor, but did it allow or inhibit innovation? The processes of change above all others have always fascinated his-torians, but to understand them you have to find out what was 'normal' at any particular time. Those are some of the problems we need to solve. The answers will not always come. Nevertheless, most buildings, the humdrum as well as the picturesque, can contribute a scrap of information. The effect is cumulative.

The earliest surviving houses in Earls Colne are hall-houses. The main living area, called the hall, was a single large room open to the roof, a feature that was present in the homes of nearly all the different social classes. The king had a hall and so did the aristocracy that served him. Beneath the aristocracy were the free peasants, the yeomanry, and many of them were also building halls towards the end of the Middle Ages in emulation of their social superiors. Even peasants who had not reached the level of yeoman sometimes built halls if they could afford to build a substantial home at all. It was, after all, a great improve-ment over the flimsy dwellings of rubble, clay and wood, lasting only a generation or so, which housed most of the peasantry at this time and continued to do so for several centuries.

We can see how peasants first built halls at Purton Green Farm, over the county boundary in Suffolk at Stansfield. It has the perfect image of the secluded English farmhouse. Its timber-framed walls and thatched roof set among trees at the bottom of a narrow lane bounded by open fields look almost eternal. Indeed, the house is remarkably ancient, perhaps even seven hundred years old. When Purton Green Farm was new, about 1280, it was not alone as it is now, but part of a thriving village called Purton Green. There were several farms here, and the lane was once the busy road that led to the fields and to the neighbouring villages of Stansfield and Depden. While Purton Green

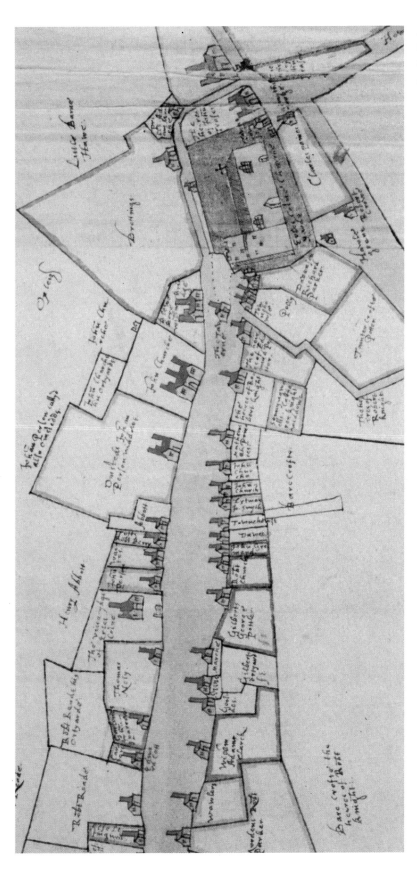

Amyce's map of Earls Colne made in 1598, showing the church, and the plots and houses that face the High Street.

Bayleaf, as re-erected at the Weald and Downland Open Air Museum in Singleton. The jettied ends and the recessed hall with its large window are clearly visible beneath the large hipped roof.

Purton Green Farm, Stansfield. The epitome of rural England at its loveliest, this house lives up to its promise by being extremely old and having one of the most interesting timber frames in the country.

is now less of a place than once it was, the house itself is more. It has grown from its original form into a more extensive house. Each stage of its growth represents a change in the needs of its occupiers. No surviving records tell us what they were, but the structure itself, its context within what we know of medieval society and the economic changes of the times all help to explain it.

Purton Green Farm was first built as little more than a large single room, the hall. Archaeological investigations have shown that halls were in use as long ago as the seventh century, and were still in use in poor parts of the country a thousand years later. The southern end of Purton Green Farm is not part of the original house, and the north end was smaller than it is now and apparently partitioned off to form a small separate space with a loft over it. This arrangement was common. By contrast, the size of the hall and the quality of workmanship were outstanding for the time. The main room is over 25 feet high to the ridge of its open roof, and it is well over 20 feet wide. This is very large for a peasant house, well out of the ordinary run of things. Indeed, it is this size taken with the high quality of carpentry used in the timber frame that allows us to call this room a hall, as it would have been by its builders and its occupants.

Size and quality of workmanship marked halls apart from the single-roomed dwellings of poor peasants, and had done so since the Dark Ages. The Old English poem *Beowulf* describes what an ancient royal hall was like. It tells of its wide arched gables, its steep gold roof, its iron-bound door and other wonders of that distant seventh-century

Purton Green Farm, Stansfield, looking across the open hall to the restored partition fitted into the aisled cross-frame. The arcade-posts are clearly visible rising above the openings to the service rooms and the stairs up to the solar.

world. More vividly the poem recounts how the hall was the scene of noble gatherings, of customary feasting and drinking to the strains of the minstrel's harp and the epic words of the bard. When finally overcome with drink, the nobles fell into a bottomless sleep, and King Hrothgar and his queen slipped away for the night to the privacy of their chamber, a *brydbur* or bower. The hall was not just a place for drunken revelry, however; it was the centre of government and justice as well as a place for banquets. It was the centre of aristocratic life.

Life itself was symbolised by the fire that burned on a great open hearth in the middle of the hall. The eighth-century English historian Bede recognised this symbol in a parable which he set in Ad Gefrin, the hall of King Edwin of Bernicia. Here he and his nobles were contemplating their conversion to Christianity in 627. A sparrow representing the human soul flies into the hall from the wintry storms outside and for a moment experiences the comfort and warmth of life around the fire before vanishing into the dark uncertainties of death outside. That very hall has been one of the major archaeological discoveries of recent years. It has given substance to Bede's parable and to the mythical hall in *Beowulf*, though only its foundations survive on the bleak hill above the Northumberland village of Yeavering that took its name.

The great hall of Penshurst Place, Kent, a far grander hall than any yeoman could afford, but it nevertheless has the same arrangement as a yeoman's house with an open fire at the centre, screened entrances at the low end and service rooms beyond.

The hall reached its peak long afterwards in the rebuilding of Westminster Hall at the command of Richard II at the end of the fourteenth century. By then the hall had become the characteristic domestic building of the Middle Ages. Its strength lay in its simplicity: a room with a fire. Size was important too. The hall had to be high so that the smoke from the fire would rise well above your head and not choke you before it drifted out of the roof through a louvre or a more simple opening, or even between the tiles or under the thatch. Height was prized because it conferred status on a building. A hall had to be long so that there was space for a formal table for feasting as far from the entrance as possible in order to impress the visitors. The table was often placed on a raised platform or dais, and this came to be known as the high end of the hall even when the table was placed directly on the ground. The low end, by distinction, was by the entrance, where the servants would bring in the food from an outside kitchen. There would be large windows by the high table, and their size was again a source of status. Before glass was common these windows were open. There would often be one each side so that when the weather was stormy the one on the windward side could be closed with shutters, while the other still let in enough light. That meant that you never added further buildings to the sides of the hall, only at its ends. The high end was also decorated with a moulded beam behind the high table or perhaps an ornate canopy extending over it. Other parts of the hall were again decorated to enhance its importance – the more prominent timbers of the roof, for instance, and the screen at the low end protecting it from draughts from the entrances.

What royalty and the aristocracy had done was good enough for yeomen, and they copied it. Feasting and drinking might be no more to yeomen than everyday meals set at a table in the glow of the open fire where the food had been cooked. The performances of the royal bards and harpers might be no more than family tales and local gossip, affairs of state no more than planning farming activities and instructing the few household servants. But for all these they needed a large open room with a fire, and so came to build halls like the king.

Purton Green Farm started as just such a hall, and is one of the oldest examples to survive. We know nothing of its first builders except that they were not manorial lords. We do not know when the house was first built except that the details of its carpentry suggest a date towards the end of the thirteenth century. What we do know is that from an early date hereabouts in Suffolk there were individual farms belonging to freeholders, and set within their own enclosed land. This central part of Suffolk has rich, clay-based soil that enabled local yeoman farmers to specialise, particularly in dairy farming. Clay soils tend to be damp, and produce the good grass that cattle need. There was a stream near Purton Green, essential to both man and beast, and not far away were markets for their produce, Bury St Edmunds to the north and a series of little towns along the River Stour to the south.

Yeomen were thriving here shortly before 1300. Not far to the east, at Combs on the southern outskirts of Stowmarket, there used to be a house called Edgar's Farm. It had a similar though more advanced form of timber framing, and may have been built early in the fourteenth century. It belonged to the Adgors, a family of yeoman farmers, and

White Cottage, Wacton, Norfolk. Above: The exterior of the building showing in the centre the large once-unglazed window at the high end of the hall and the entrance at the low end. These are flanked by a window on the left for the chamber and another window on the right for one of the service rooms. The upper windows light the lofts above. Apart from the windows and doorway, there is nothing on the front of the house to indicate what the internal arrangements are. The lean-to on the left and the extension to the rear on the right are modern. Right: The interior of the open hall showing the front entrance on the right, the twin doors to the service rooms in the centre and the back door on the left. Spanning the hall is the arch of the open, central cross-frame.

was perhaps built by John and Ascelina Adgor who were buying land around Combs in 1342 and 1346. Part of the house can still be seen in Stowmarket in its rebuilt form at the Museum of East Anglian Life. Edgar's Farm offers tentative support to the possible origin of Purton Green Farm as being the house of another yeoman that was built perhaps fifty years earlier.

How were these two farmhouses built? The clay soil of Suffolk and Essex not only helped the dairyman but also provided the best conditions for oak trees to grow. Oak is the king not just of the forest but of all native building timbers. Most halls were built of it. For hardness and durability, for resistance to warping and splitting it is supreme. Since prehistoric times woodmen had cultivated oak and other trees by a regular process of cropping, known as coppicing, in order to provide straight timber that could be used for building. Without this cultivation the natural oak forests would have been depleted long before the end of the Middle Ages so great was the demand for timber. A house like Purton Green Farm could easily use up to a hundred trunks for its frame and more would be needed for lesser parts.

Next in the building process came the carpenters. Their traditions were not so old, but were now developing fast. Only in the preceding century or so had they discovered how to make buildings last. Previously, timber buildings had been made firm by burying the bottom end of their upright posts in the ground to give them stability, and the upper parts, including the roof timbers, were joined together in a relatively unsophisticated way. The great disadvantage of doing this was that because the posts were set in the earth they soon rotted, as every owner of a wooden garden fence will know. Once that had happened the building was doomed. By about 1200, carpenters had learned how to brace a frame well enough to give it adequate rigidity without having to sink the main posts in the earth. Instead, they rested them above the ground on a low plinth and perhaps a timber sill. They

Building a timber-framed house in the fifteenth century. There is much artistic licence in this medieval illustration, as timbers were usually cut in carpenters' yards, not on site, and the framing as shown is unlike any found in England which date from that time.

could then be kept dry enough not to rot. As far as we know, the carpenters developed these skills by building a number of huge barns that were used to house the large crops of grain grown on the great monastic estates. Soon, perhaps at the same time, their skills were employed in manor houses, some belonging to the Church, but ones belonging to laymen were involved as well. Like other building craftsmen, the carpenters belonged to a guild which carefully regulated entry to the craft and how apprentices should learn it from masters. We do not know for certain if there was any difference between those who worked on the most important buildings, perhaps raising wide roofs over cathedrals, and those who sold their skills to a few free peasants to provide and to erect the frames of their halls. What we do know is that by the end of the thirteenth century these skills were now available to yeomen like the one who built Purton Green Farm.

Their buildings were prefabricated. This is by no means a modern development. The timbers were cut to shape in the carpenters' yard to a predetermined design and size, and then taken to the site for erection. Raising the frame into position would take only a few days. But completing the walls by filling them with a basketwork of wattles and covering them with a daub of clay or earth mixed with straw and hair took several weeks. The house was built to a high quality and to a standard of design that only skilled craftsmen could provide. That is why it has lasted so long. The overall design of the framing was part of the craftsman's skill, and he probably knew no other. It was central to his tradition. All the yeoman could do was to choose the size of his house and how many rooms it should have within very small limits.

The yeoman who commanded the building of Purton Green Farm not only used skilled craftsmen, but also built it in the form of an aisled hall. At this time, large barns and wide royal halls had to have internal posts, known as arcade posts, to support the roof. They notionally divided the interior into a nave and aisles like a church. The posts were a structural necessity, though in halls they did tend to get in the way. Because wide royal halls had them, manorial halls followed suit, and internal posts and aisles took on connotations of status, even though the aisles might be very narrow. The same happened at Purton Green Farm. Moreover, the posts are decorated with carved capitals just above head height, just as you would see them in a manorial hall or in church – another example of how ideas and skills moved down society and entered the vernacular building tradition.

Purton Green Farm took yet another feature of buildings higher up the social scale. King Hrothgar in the poem *Beowulf* had a separate building near his hall called a 'bower', which he used as a sleeping room. Soon bowers were attached to halls for the sake of convenience. In many of the manor houses built in Essex and Suffolk in the thirteenth century and shortly afterwards one end of the hall was partitioned off. This was normally the end furthest from the high table and was called the low end of the hall. Here a floor was inserted, dividing the partitioned end into two storeys. The ground-floor room was used as a store or service room for food, which could also be prepared there before it was taken to be cooked over the open fire in the hall. The upper room could be used as a private bedroom or bower. This Old English word was soon ousted in the South of England by the more fashionable Anglo-

A carved capital on one of the arcade-posts at Purton Green Farm, Stansfield. This is a form of architectural decoration often used in timber-framed hall-houses.

French words 'chamber' and 'solar'. A chamber was any private room, but a solar was always an upper room, the word deriving from the Latin *sol* for sun, because in ancient times solars were open to the sky.

This arrangement of hall and partitioned end of two storeys with a solar or bower became common among the peasantry of the south-eastern part of England by the end of the fourteenth century. The word 'hall' itself was used for ever smaller rooms. In the 1380s Chaucer was talking of the hall of one comparatively poor person, the poor widow of the *Nun's priest's tale*. She was what today we would call a smallholder. Her income came from a little land and a few animals – three large sows, three cows, a sheep, and a cock and some hens. Chaucer described her 'dwelling in a narrow cottage, beside a grove, in a dale' with her two daughters. The house was already old at the time of Chaucer's tale, and divided into two parts like Purton Green Farm: 'Full sooty was her bower and so was her hall.' The soot was caused by the smoke that drifted up from the open fire into the roof and coated the rafters. It cannot have been too choking because up here her hens perched to roost.

Surprisingly enough these open fires did not always make a house filthy and choking. Chaucer's contemporary, the poet Langland, said that a man had three things to fear at home. One was a wicked wife with a sharp tongue, the second was a fallen tile from the roof that would let the rain in on his bed, the third a smoky, smouldering fire that made him bleary-eyed and hoarse in the throat. Langland saw no reason for a man to suffer any of these three, and for them to do so was a real misfortune.

It seems that people were less concerned with cleanliness, though the evidence is confusing. At the start of the sixteenth century the Dutch scholar and traveller Erasmus was outraged by the chronic filth in the Englishman's home.

> The floors are all of clay, and moreover rushes from marshes are so repeatedly renewed that the foundation often remains for twenty years, harbouring down there spittle and vomit, dogs' and men's urine, spilt beer and the remains of fish and other unspeakable filth.

There was certainly cause for complaint. Filth meant rats, rats meant the plague, and plague meant death. Nevertheless, archaeologists have been constantly impressed in their investigations of ruined medieval houses by how their clay floors have been scoured by constant sweeping. 'First sweep thy house, dress up thy dishboard and set all things in good order,' advised the sixteenth-century writer John Fitzherbert. Perhaps more housewives heeded his list of daily chores than Erasmus realised.

The privacy that a bower offered a king was not yet shared by the peasantry. Chaucer's poor widow and her two daughters probably slept in theirs together, perhaps in the same bed. Chaucer's miller of Trumpington and his wife shared their chamber with their plump daughter of twenty summers, though she had a bed of her own, and there was a cradle for a baby son. The only privacy here came with nocturnal darkness. When two students begged shelter for the night,

A peasant's house in a scene from the Bayeux Tapestry, being set on fire by William's soldiers in 1066. The top half shows the outside of the house, the bottom half a woman and child inside it trying to escape.

another bed was set up in the chamber for them. There followed the first and best bedroom farce in English literature, and the bawdiest. Chaucer cannot have wanted his reader to take it too seriously, but the serious historian cannot mistake the implication that bowers or chambers were used as communal bedrooms.

We know little of family structure in the Middle Ages, but it seems to have been similar to what we know three hundred years later when records are clearer on this point. A boy and a girl might be lovers, but their hope of legal consummation was only fulfilled if they could set up home and become a housebondman – a husband – and a housewife. They were then recognised in common law. Economic necessity and the teaching of the Church through the Catechism constantly tempered romance and delayed marriage until late in what were often short lives.

To set up home meant acquiring land. In places where the land hunger of the late thirteenth century was most acute, young men deliberately sought out widows with land as marriage partners – and the older they were the better. That way they might soon die and the men would still be young enough to marry again and start a family. Late marriage meant small families, and high mortality made them smaller. A household with three generations living in it was fairly rare.

An affluent household, as the one at Purton Green must have been, usually had a few servants. These were teenage children who had been sent out from their own homes to learn all the aspects of rural life, both about the house and about the farm, before they became householders themselves. They seem to have been treated as equals within the family circle, and a yeoman would as readily call a servant his son as he would his own heir. Nevertheless, over the years these servants would move from family to family within a radius of a dozen or so miles until at last they came into an inheritance, or had saved enough to acquire land, or perhaps found a marriage partner who could take them out of their servitude.

Over the years there were several changes at Purton Green Farm, and they were typical of many other hall-houses. The first change was to make a much larger solar and service space at the low end of the hall. The enlarged ground floor was now big enough to be divided into two rooms. One was probably for dry food, for storing grain and flour, and the bread made from it. This room would have been called a pantry, after the French word *pain* for bread. The second service room, probably the cooler one in the north-east corner, could have been used for storing liquids, like milk from the farm, the ale made from the farm's barley and cider from its apples. It would have been called a buttery, nothing to do with butter, but a corruption of the French *bouteillerie*, a bottle store. Even with this much storage space, there is little doubt that the enlarged bower or solar overhead would have been used as a store for farm produce as well as a bedroom. Although the master and his wife could well have had their bed up here – perhaps the only bed in the house – it would have been surrounded with jars or bins of grain, apples and cheeses, and perhaps the more valuable farm implements. A chest or two would have been enough for their clothing and bedding.

At a later date there were further changes. The owner abandoned this solar and built a complete new chamber at the other end of the hall – that is, beyond the high end. This again conformed with a pattern of

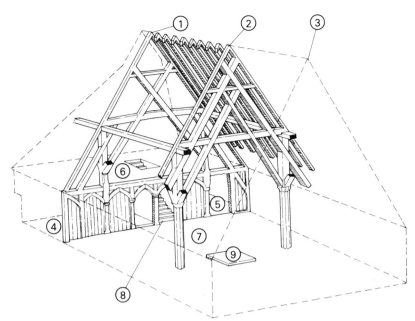

Perspective view of part of the timber frame of Purton Green Farm, after the extension to form larger service rooms and solar. (1) Aisled cross-frame between hall and service rooms; (2) Aisled cross-frame with free-standing arcade-posts; (3) Approximate southern end of building; (4) Pantry; (5) Buttery; (6) Solar; (7) Hall; (8) Stairs to solar; (9) Open hearth.

building already established in manor houses where the hall was now flanked by a service block and a chamber block, one at each end. In this way the windows of the hall remained unimpeded, and the characteristic medieval three-part plan of service, hall and chamber was established. With it came the hierarchy important in the manor house, the lord at the high end and the servants at the low end of the house. Yet there is no evidence to suggest that this mattered to the yeoman. However closely he copied the manor in the form of his house he did not extend this to his relationship with his servants. This was because he and his wife worked beside them all round the house and the farm. Two features alone were likely to separate master and servants and emphasise his role as head of the household. He and his wife might sit on chairs at the hall table, while the rest of the family, servants included, would make do with benches. Furthermore, he and his wife might sleep together alone in their private chamber, despite the example of Chaucer's miller of Trumpington. The rest of the household would have rougher beds in the upper rooms or even in the hall.

The additions at Purton Green Farm were made in the later Middle Ages, the fifteenth and early sixteenth centuries. By then substantial hall-houses like this were no longer rare. Thirty years ago historians had identified practically no peasant halls built before 1350, and only a few hundred were known to date from the following two centuries. Today these numbers have greatly increased, but still the middle of the fourteenth century seems to be a divide. This is not simply because few houses have lasted from before this time, though constructional methods were definitely improving and giving houses a greater chance of survival; nor is it because historians find it difficult to identify early houses for what they are. The main reason is that events in the fourteenth century radically changed society and gave peasants a chance to become rich and put their money into substantial houses.

In the thirteenth century there was a numerous and still growing population largely controlled by strong manors. Grain was generally the most efficient way of obtaining food from the land. So land was everywhere going under the plough to provide food, though often that was an unproductive use as not all land was suited to grain. In the second decade of the fourteenth century there were terrible famines. For two years running bad weather ruined the harvest and filled the countryside with corpses. In 1348 the Black Death reached England. It cut down a third of the population at a stroke. It was the greatest calamity in English history, the turning point of the Middle Ages. The plague returned in 1361–1362, and kept returning to pick off yet more people for another three hundred years. By 1500 the population was at half its peak level of the thirteenth century. Despite the suffering, despite the millions of personal catastrophes, one good thing came out of the plague. It undermined the old social order. It brought freedom and wealth to many of those peasants whom it chose to spare. At the same time, the power of the old landowners was curbed if not destroyed. Land became a glut on the market, labour scarce. King and government – that is, the landowners – tried to fix wages at their level before the plague. They roundly condemned the peasantry for exploiting this new-found economic strength and failing to work in the manorial fields. The consequent Peasants' Revolt of 1381 was eventually suppressed, but many landowners gave up the struggle to keep the peasantry in their place. Increasingly they leased out their land for a fixed rent, and left it to the peasant leaseholders to take the economic initiative, and the profits.

The peasantry did this with mixed success. Arable farming remained difficult as it was labour intensive and needed a large degree of organisation. In the great corn-growing counties of England, the South, the Midlands and the North-east, manorial control kept some semblance of its past authority, so not all the peasantry broke free and prospered. Some landowners reacted to the changed economic circumstances by turning their land into great sheep runs and destroying what remained of peasant villages in the process. But in the South-east and East Anglia, and in the West and North, pastoral farming had been more important. With less need of labour and often with weaker manorial control, now tending to be weaker still, the peasantry found themselves in a good position to exploit their chance of freedom. Many of them had the time to combine farming with other activities. In the Weald of Kent, where yeoman farmers had been free from ancient times, cattle farming was the principal means of exploiting the rather poor soil. That left plenty of time for yeomen to set up in a variety of industries. Good supplies of water allowed them to manufacture cloth, so they became clothiers, buying in their wool from flocks on the nearby Romney Marsh and the South Downs. They exploited the tannin that came from the bark of their oak trees and, using the hides from their cattle, became tanners. Their wealth, moreover, did not fall into ever fewer hands. In Kent a system of partible inheritance called 'gavelkind' traditionally gave a share of a man's land to all his heirs, not just the eldest. This made it difficult for the first-born of a family to build up a large estate over several generations. Instead, there was a constant exchange of land from one hand to another, keeping everyone on their toes to exploit it as best they could. By the end of the Middle Ages the yeomen of Kent were proverbially the richest in the kingdom (although nobody could become wealthy enough to enter the ranks of the aristocracy). Because there were so many of these rich yeomen, they were able to build the greatest concentration of fine medieval houses in England and probably in all Europe.

While Kent's peasantry built on this lavish scale, yeomen in other parts of the country followed on a smaller scale or at a later date. By the end of the Middle Ages the peasantry were an exceedingly varied class. The wealthiest were nudging their way into the gentry. These were the aspiring yeomen. The poorest, the landless labourers, still led lives so abject that the future for each family was a lottery between starvation and servitude. For most people, life was like a relentless game of snakes and ladders, played with their health, the vicissitudes of the weather and their abilities to husband the soil, even though the dice were now slightly loaded in their favour.

The poorest continued to live in rough houses of one or two and occasionally three rooms as they had done for centuries. They were built of mud, sometimes with flimsy pieces of wood to support their walls, or of flint or rubble bound by soft, crumbly mortar, or whatever else came cheaply to hand. In some places the lords of the manors would grant their tenants a few pieces of solid timber to provide a decent frame for walls and roof, and these houses were more likely to survive. In many parts of the country (except for the South-east and East) these might be curved or elbowed timbers called 'crucks'. They were joined to form an A-shaped frame that curved outwards to support the junction between the walls and the roof. Three or four cruck frames or trusses set in a row provided a comparatively simple means of framing a house.

The origin of this seemingly primitive method of framing is obscure. Like so much in vernacular building, the cruck truss appears to have been invented not by the peasantry but higher in society, and to have come down to them from the grander halls of the aristocracy. Indeed, the earliest cruck-framed houses of the peasantry are substantial halls even though they are small. They have been found in villages like Steventon and Harwell in the fertile Thames valley near Oxford, where peasants suffered little interference from the lords of the manors and had the great advantage of secure tenancies of their land. They built low halls, because high ones would need inordinately long and expensive timbers for the cruck trusses. Despite their small size they were often flanked by a service room and a chamber just like a manor house.

In many parts of the country the service end was not used domestically, but served an agricultural function. This is hard to prove now, because survivors have been converted to modern uses. However, in the more westerly and northerly pastoral areas the service room often had a drain running down its centre towards the end wall. This is conclusive evidence that the room was used for cattle, the drain carrying away their urine. A hall linked directly to a cow-house or cattle-shed is called a 'long-house'. These houses have the appearance of length because they are often low and narrow; their builders were seldom rich enough to build larger houses.

A hall-house in the Weald of Kent may be just as long or longer, but it will not look it because it is broader and much higher. It never

A cruck truss supporting the walls and roof of a barn recorded by John Buckler early in the nineteenth century at Drayton, Oxfordshire.

A Devon long-house: Sanders at Lettaford, a hamlet of North Bovey, close to the edge of Dartmoor. The house has been altered since it was built in about 1500 with an open hall, but the wide entrance common to man and beast is clearly visible between the house on the left and the shippon, West Country dialect for a cow-house, on the right.

functioned as a long-house with a cattle-shed, even though the farmers here were equally involved with cattle. They differed in two significant ways from other pastoral farmers. They did not bring their cattle indoors during the winter, but kept them in open yards or in low shelters, often attached to their barns, which they called 'lodges'. And they were much richer. Consequently, they built hall-houses with service rooms that were for domestic not agricultural uses and never for housing cattle. Because these yeomen were so rich, their halls were correspondingly large. They could easily be 25 to 30 feet high, enough to fit in three of today's storeys and then a comfortable loft.

These yeomen were able to profit from the advances in carpentry made during the thirteenth century, when Purton Green Farm was built. Rather than using cruck trusses, they exploited a method of timber framing that built up a house from a series of horizontal and vertical timbers which formed a box with a roof placed on top. The most significant development for the box frame was the invention of an efficient joint that held the top of a vertical post to both the horizontal beam or plate running down the length of the building beneath the roof, and the tie-beam that ran across the building and tied the two sides of the frame together. This junction was especially important because it also had to bear the weight of the roof rafters. The combination of mortises and tenons and dovetails is like a Chinese puzzle, but this joint was so efficient that from its development in the later thirteenth century to the end of the use of oak as a major building material five hundred years later it remained unchanged. It made the use of aisles redundant in any span of less than about 20 feet, so they and the internal posts that went with them fell out of use, notwithstanding their former connotations of status. Carpenters could now frame a building with far fewer timbers. At the same time they developed a number of regional traditions of timber framing as more and more yeomen came to employ them to build substantial houses.

Many hall-houses in Kent have the form of huge timber boxes. Over them are immense roofs. Instead of vertical gables at each end, the ends slope downwards to form what are called 'hips'. They greatly improve the stability of the roof under the pressure of the wind and its own weight. In the centre of the house is a large open hall, now usually modernised with a chimney-stack and filled in with inserted floors. It is flanked by service rooms and a chamber in the usual way, both with rooms above. These upper rooms often project on the outside by a couple of feet. They are supported by their floor joists, which jut out to form what is called a 'jetty'. Jetties seem to have originated in towns where restricted building land made the extra space provided by a jettied upper floor particularly valuable. They came about because it is easier to fix floor joists into an already assembled timber frame than to make their fixture part of the primary assembly process. Therefore one end of the joist is first fixed by tenoning it into an already assembled cross-beam. Then, as the other end could never also be tenoned into a second assembled cross-beam, it is simply allowed to rest on this second beam. By projecting the joists outwards to form a jetty they can be more firmly positioned and the upper floor can be made a little larger than the one beneath. The jetty has the further advantage of advertising the presence of the upper floor. When upper floors were still fairly rare, as they were in the Middle Ages, this advertisement added to the status of the building. So jetties soon became fashionable and were taken up elsewhere in the countryside.

At first the jetties in Kent hall-houses were at one of the ends. But they were not easily seen there, and towards the end of the fourteenth century it became common to put the jetties at the front, where their presence was more obvious. So the hall came to be flanked by end blocks with upper rooms projecting on jetties. The large hipped roof ran down to the eaves line of the projecting upper rooms and bridged the gap between them along the front of the hall, usually with two curved braces to support it. The effect of the jettied ends and the overhanging roof was to leave the hall recessed behind them.

This arrangement of the hall-house is characteristic of Kent, and of Sussex too. It has given rise to the term 'Wealden hall', though the type is found outside the Weald and there are a few examples right outside the South-east as far away as Herefordshire and Yorkshire. Architecturally, it is an extremely expressive design. The storeyed ends are emphasised by the jetties, the open hall between them by its recessed position and, if it has not been altered, by the large window that lit the table at the high end.

Wealden halls were built in great numbers. Several hundred are known in Kent and Sussex, and some villages have three or four of them each. Their history has yet to be written, and in some ways we know remarkably little of their origin. The design was becoming popular well before 1400, thanks to the great wealth of local yeomen, but its origin can only be guessed at.

Although the design integrates the three parts – hall, service and chamber – in a particularly satisfying way, yeomen seem to have been happy to build them in sections if their finances could not stretch to a complete house. An example is the well-known Wealden hall called Bayleaf Farm at Boughbeech near Chiddingstone in Kent. Because its

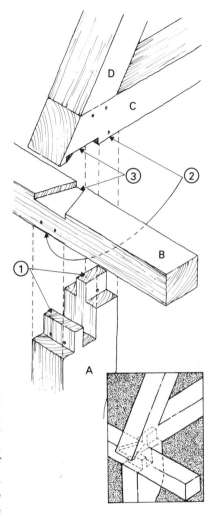

Standard method of joining main-post, wall-plate, tie-beam and rafter, as devised about 1300. A: Main-post; B: Wall-plate; C: Tie-beam; D: Rafter. (1) Tenons; (2) Mortises (slots) underneath B and C; (3) Dovetail.

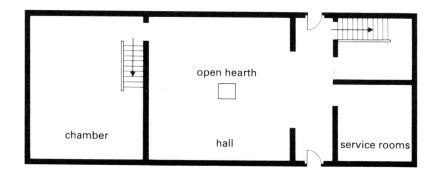

The plan of a hall-house like Bayleaf. The hall is open to the roof to allow the smoke from the fire to escape, but the chamber and service rooms may be floored over to provide extra accommodation above.

site was needed for a reservoir, the house was taken down, timber by timber, and rebuilt at the Weald and Downland Open Air Museum at Singleton. The ensuing study of its frame and the documents that relate to Chiddingstone show that the chamber end was not part of the first build. The hall and service rooms together with the room over them were built first, all of a piece, shortly after 1400, probably by Henry Bayly. He was nominally a tenant of the manor of Sundridge and paid the paltry rent of 3*d* or 9*d* a quarter and a hen or some eggs for his land. The house he built stood on the cold clay soil below the Weald of Kent. It is by no means good soil agriculturally, but Bayly had enough for his needs.

In the house that bears a name based on his own he showed how well the yeomen of Kent were doing fifty years after the Black Death and a mere twenty after the Peasants' Revolt.

He probably used his house like the owners of Purton Green Farm, with a hall and a private chamber in the solar over the pair of service rooms. It was not until about 1510 that a successor to the Bayly family completed the house by adding the chamber at the high end of the hall, again with an upper room. The remarkable thing is how consistently the new end conforms to the design of the old, despite the century that elapsed between them, and the new generation of craftsmen who built it. So the aesthetic value of the design was clearly prized by the yeomen and craftsmen who built these halls. If you were building on as large a scale as this you would not be concerned with utility alone. In fact, it is hard to find even a poor hall where no attention has been paid to aesthetic values.

In other parts of the country there was less money for such a show. In Essex and elsewhere hall-houses had a different overall form and the roof-line was more varied. The halls themselves were usually lower than in Kent and did not reach the height needed by the storeyed chamber and service rooms. These end rooms were then treated as cross wings and given separate, higher roofs, often emphasised by gables facing the front. The unifying effect of the unbroken roof of the Wealden hall was thus lost and the ability to throw off rainwater was reduced, but the roof-line was more varied and picturesque.

It is typical of the developing traditions of craftsmanship around the country that a basic three-part plan could be treated in so many different ways and made to produce so many apparently dissimilar houses. In the West Midlands many hall-houses had a gabled wing at only one end, and a floor had to be inserted into the other end without any architectural emphasis. Often these halls had cruck trusses rather

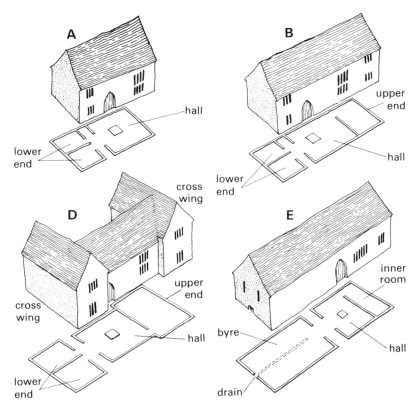

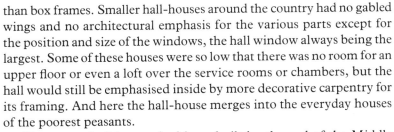

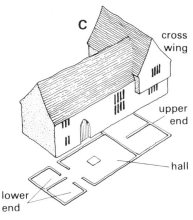

*Five forms of hall-houses.
A: Hall and service room with
solar over it, as in second stage of
Purton Green Farm. B: All
rooms in line under continuous
roof. C: Single cross-wing, jettied
out at front, for chamber with
solar above it. D: Two-storeyed
cross-wings at both ends for
service rooms and chamber.
E: Byre or cow-house at lower
end and inner room combining
functions of chamber and service
rooms at higher end, thus forming
a long-house.*

than box frames. Smaller hall-houses around the country had no gabled wings and no architectural emphasis for the various parts except for the position and size of the windows, the hall window always being the largest. Some of these houses were so low that there was no room for an upper floor or even a loft over the service rooms or chambers, but the hall would still be emphasised inside by more decorative carpentry for its framing. And here the hall-house merges into the everyday houses of the poorest peasants.

How many hall-houses had been built by the end of the Middle Ages is hard to guess. There may be 2000 of them in Kent, two or three times as many in the Home Counties and a few more thousand in the rest of the country. In the well-preserved Sussex township of Robertsbridge the architectural historians David and Barbara Martin have estimated that a quarter of the forty-eight halls of the Middle Ages still remain today. At a guess, using these figures we can imagine that there might have been 100 000 or even 200 000 hall-houses around England by the end of the Middle Ages, and that they accommodated just possibly a quarter or a third of the population of about 3 million. Only one conclusion may be drawn from this guesswork, but it is significant. A substantial part of the population lived in houses that were tolerably spacious and comfortable, that provided separate rooms for working, living and sleeping, albeit with little privacy, and that did not need to be rebuilt every generation. Indeed, these houses were so well built that they lasted far longer than their builders expected.

The yeomen of the fourteenth and fifteenth centuries began the Great Rebuilding of rural England, as Professor W G Hoskins, author of *The Making of the English Landscape*, termed it. He undertook his

Variations in the design of hall-houses.
Above: Blackwell Farm at Latimer in Buckinghamshire has both ends differentiated by wings.
Right: Walnut Tree Farm at Luffenhall, Weston, Hertfordshire, has a single end differentiated with a jettied wing.

research into this subject thirty years ago. Being unaware of the extent of medieval halls he believed that the rebuilding that produced the England we see today began in Queen Elizabeth's reign, and he associated its start with the great prosperity of her times. Today we recognise instead the paradox that English yeomen started the process at a time when the population was in decline and wherever you looked you saw the plague. Although the plague changed society and freed the peasantry with the result that some could build these new substantial houses, we can also see that such houses provided domestic conditions decent enough perhaps to deter the rats that carried the fleas that scattered the plague.

The end of the plague in 1665 was still a long way in the future, and by that time houses had become very different. Even then people did not understand the connection between disease and poor housing. What they did understand, and had done since the later Middle Ages, was that they did not have to have the inordinate wealth of the aristocracy to build a good house. With luck, persistence and hard work, a sizeable minority might enter the middling rank of the yeomanry if they lived in the right part of the country, and the best thing they could spend their money on then was a good home.

Spring Cottage, once the hall-house of a prosperous Yetminster yeoman and then progressively modernised to include an enclosed hearth and chimney-stack.

The enclosed hearth at Spring Cottage seen through the doorway in the partition separating the chamber from the formerly open hall.

From the sixteenth century right through Thomas Hardy's time to the present day herds of milking cattle have been the basis of Yetminster's wealth.

CHAPTER TWO
The Fireside Revolution

Forty years ago no child would ever draw a house without a chimney. It was essential not just to the working of the house, but to its image as well. A door, a window, a roof and a chimney, preferably with some smoke to indicate the comfort of a hearth – that is all you needed. Today things are different. After four hundred years the chimney is coming to the end of its usefulness.

When Queen Elizabeth I came to the throne in 1558 most people still did not have a chimney. They were an unusual luxury, but they were beginning to spread. A substantial class of yeomen was living in solid hall-houses. In wealthy Kent there were now many halls of prodigious size, showing how affluent a favoured section of the peasantry had become in the last two centuries of the Middle Ages. But open halls had been decreasing in size for some while. This was not through any decline in the economic conditions of the peasantry. If anything, their wealth was to continue to grow until well into the seventeenth century. Instead, the hall was slowly becoming obsolete. A Wealden hall-house could easily contain six rooms. Its central room or hall remained important, but the secondary rooms took over more and more of its functions as everyday living and working rooms. In addition, the benefit of increased storage space upstairs began to erode the usefulness of the open hall. Often half of it was floored over, providing much more space upstairs at little cost. There was still half left open to provide a way for the smoke to reach the roof from the open hearth.

This was a halfway stage to a much more important innovation. If you enclosed your fire in a brick or stone chimney-stack, the open hall

Yetminster chimneys, Dorset. They are no surprise in the twentieth century but they represented a real revolution in the sixteenth century.

Yetminster houses: some of the many houses built at the end of the sixteenth century and early in the seventeenth with chimney-stacks and continuous upper floors. To this day they reflect the great wealth of the local yeomen at that time.

became completely redundant and you could have a continuous upper floor from one end of your house to the other, running over the chamber and service ends and over the hall. You also had a potentially much cleaner house. This was the fireside revolution.

Of course chimney-stacks were occasionally used in the later Middle Ages, especially among the rich and in towns where there was no space for open halls. But chimney-stacks were not widespread. Yeomen started to build them in any number only in the sixteenth century, as William Harrison, rector of Radwinter, noted in the 1570s. He was particularly struck by how everyone was building them in Essex, his part of the country. 'There are old men yet dwelling in the village where I remain which have noted three things to be marvellously altered in England within their sound remembrance,' he wrote in his *Description of England*:

One is the multitude of chimneys lately erected, whereas in their young days there were not above two or three, if so many . . . but each one made his fire against a reredos in the hall, where he dined and dressed his meat . . . the second is the great . . . amendment of lodging. . . . The third . . . is the exchange of vessel, as of treen platters into pewter, and wooden spoons into silver or tin.

The enclosed hearth and its chimney-stack were innovations that brought extra space, comfort and convenience. The open hall became a thing of the past. With developing building skills and increasing wealth, first the yeoman farmers and their like, then the poorer husbandmen, and finally, after about two hundred years, the landless labourers built their houses with chimney-stacks. Eventually, a house might have several enclosed hearths in one or more chimney-stacks as they became cheaper to build. That allowed what Harrison called the 'amendment of lodging', the increase in the number of rooms you could use for special functions, and also the number of them with hearths. Your house could be more comfortable now, and more private – though it was some time before this mattered. The idea of privacy developed very slowly.

The third thing that Harrison saw 'marvellously altered' was the great increase in houshold goods that people owned, and the change in their quality. The wooden bowls and plates of the past were now of pewter, wooden spoons now of silver. It was another expression of the new wealth that made this great investment in houses possible. Contemporary documents bear out Harrison's words, and open a window on these houses and the lives of those men and women who lived in them. There are manorial rolls, the occasional building contract, wills and, above all, inventories. These were the lists of personal possessions, recorded room by room. Ecclesiastical law required an inventory to be made before a will could take effect or be proved.

One further improvement that Harrison would have mentioned had he been writing a few years later was the glazing of windows. At the end of the sixteenth century yeomen could at last afford glass. It made windows weathertight for the first time. Glazed windows and the new chimney-stacks allowed changes to be introduced in the planning of houses. But, as always with innovations, glass was at first a fashionable novelty. Some houses boasted far more extensively glazed windows than were strictly necessary. They became a status symbol, just as tall decorated chimney-stacks were. Both proclaimed the wealth and modernity of the householder, and helped him to rise in the esteem of his neighbours.

It was Harrison's Essex and the neighbouring counties of East Anglia and the South-east, notably Kent, that first experienced the fireside revolution. The continuing wealth of the yeomen there gave them the money to build. The substantial hall-houses they had built in every parish were now given chimney-stacks and remodelled with continuous upper floors. Here too they built the first of the new houses with chimney-stacks, and this set the pattern. Thomas Paycocke's father, for instance, was building his son a house with a chimney-stack at Great Coggeshall before 1505. It is one of the oldest surviving houses of its kind belonging to the rich group of yeomen farmers, traders and

Thomas Paycocke's house at Coggeshall in Essex, built shortly before 1505 with an enclosed hearth and chimney-stack as an original feature. The timber frame has recently been lime-washed, as it originally may have been, so it appears rather lighter than the infilling of brick nogging.

craftsmen who, two centuries before, had been faceless peasantry. Other similar houses joined Paycocke's. As early as 1490 John Grangeman of Borden in Kent bequeathed to his wife Alice the use of a room in his house that he called 'the Chimney Chambyre'. To have such a room was remarkable at that date, so much so that Grangeman could think of no better term to describe it. It was some while before there were new names for the new rooms. A building contract, rare for 1500, provided for the building of a new house with 'a chimney with 2 fyres' at Cranbrook. This was an especially rich parish in the Weald of Kent whose wealth had for ages come from cattle farms and was now greatly augmented by the highly prosperous weaving industry. It was exactly the kind of place where you would expect innovations in house building.

The fireside revolution slowly established itself in the sixteenth century and spread to other parts of England. Demand for the bricks from which chimneys were made fostered local brick-making wherever there was good brick-earth or clay, and brought down prices. In other regions a similar demand also brought local stone within the reach of an aspiring class of yeomen. Stone had been so expensive to quarry and to cut that its use was previously confined to the Church and the aristocracy. Wealthy yeomen now began to demand stone, and local quarries were opened up and exploited to provide for their houses. In some parts of the country where good building stone was plentiful every village had its quarry and a few quarrymen and masons who served its needs. In very hilly country like Dartmoor and the Pennines, stone was there for the taking on the surface or in outcrops on a yeoman's land. All he needed was the money to pay a mason and some labourers to work it for him and build his house.

These yeomen were helped by the great Tudor price rise. Their major outgoing was the cost of their land. Often they owned it outright, and, if they leased it, the rents were often low and had been fixed long beforehand. The wages they paid to their servants and to other employees certainly rose, and rents did a bit too, but these costs lagged behind the rise in the prices they obtained when they came to sell their produce. The landed peasantry did very well out of the inflation. Their poorer, landless neighbours were dependent on their wages and consequently suffered.

It was this increasing wealth combined with secure tenure of their land, not just for their own lifetime but for that of their descendants as well, that gave yeomen their incentive to build. It did not happen everywhere at once. In parts of the North an inhospitable climate and often infertile land conspired to limit wealth so much that people did not start to build houses of the new type for some two centuries. In other regions, notably parts of the Midlands where manorial control of the land was still strong, the peasant landholders were generally poorer than their brethren in the South-east and less sure of their ability to bequeath their farms to their children. They too could not afford to build these new houses with their enclosed hearths for some time. When they did so, their houses were generally smaller, just as their personal wealth was also less. You can still see evidence for the Great Rebuilding of rural England in every part of the country. In some parts the rebuilding was on a large scale; in others it hardly happened. Sometimes it started at an early date; at others it was long delayed. It all depended on money and confidence in the future. Every region of the country has its own story to tell.

The domestic architecture of the English middling people (those who lay between the poor peasant and the gentry and aristocracy) has never before or afterwards had the rich variety of local styles that it displayed in the sixteenth and seventeenth centuries. Each region had its own particular materials at its disposal as well as different sources of wealth and forms of landholding. This led to a great variety of house plans as builders responded to the challenge of where to put the new chimney-stacks. This variety appears throughout the country, region by region. There are other local differences too, such as in the subtle variations between one quarry and its neighbour serving the next village. Variations appear generation by generation as innovations were adopted, and village by village as the better favoured leaped forward, leaving the poorer to follow as best they could.

Local studies have illustrated this in a number of places around the country. A good example is the study of Yetminster in the north of Dorset by Bob Machin of Bristol University. Here as many as forty-six houses survive from before 1714 (that is, from before the Georgian period), and, even more unusual, there are many surviving documents that relate to them.

Yetminster lies on the western edge of the rich Vale of Blackmoor. It is old-established butter country, a farming region noted for its dairies, rather than for the wide-open cornfields of the higher and drier land that surrounds it. Two-thirds of the land was never ploughed and remained as permanent grassland for herds of cattle, especially the native 'Dorset horn'. A farm of any size had apple orchards and made cider. In his great novel *Tess of the d'Urbervilles*, Thomas Hardy made a point of the contrast between rich Blackmoor (he called it the Vale of the Little Dairies) and the cornland of the surrounding hills.

> Here, in the valley, the world seems to be constructed upon a smaller and more delicate scale; the fields are mere paddocks, so reduced that their hedgerows appear a network of dark green threads over-spreading the paler green of the grass. . . . Arable lands are few and limited . . . the prospect is a broad rich mass of grass and trees.

Yetminster was lucky. Its land was not just fertile and lush, but remarkably free from control by the large landowners who were in evidence elsewhere in the county. Yetminster was divided among four manors, and its inhabitants, by an accident of history, paid a very low rent for their land. These manors belonged to Salisbury Cathedral, and provided an income for its clergy. By the sixteenth century the manors had been leased or farmed out, so giving us our modern word 'farm'. This guaranteed the cathedral a fixed income rather than the variable income that might come from the profits of agriculture. These lessees also hoped for a profit and did not occupy the manors themselves, but let them out at a fixed rent to tenants – the local yeomen. The profits they won from the land soon rose through inflation much above the rents they paid. The lessees became the next best thing to freeholders, as they were entitled to pass their land on to the next generation by the payment of a small fee or fine. This custom of the manor was legally binding and gave Yetminster's yeomen complete security of tenure.

The Yetminster farmers were lucky to be in dairy farming. By the end of the sixteenth century large markets were growing for luxury commodities like butter and cheese, and demand kept ahead of supply. Grain, by contrast, was a variable crop. A good summer brought a bumper harvest. But that could mean glut and tumbling prices and profits. A bad summer meant scarcity and high prices, but there was not necessarily enough grain saved by the harvest to bring in a great profit for many farmers. Dairy products tended to benefit from both kinds of seasons. A good harvest and low grain prices gave consumers the extra money to spend on luxuries like butter and cheese, and the dairy farmers might buy in cheap grain for winter fodder for their cattle. On the other hand, wet summers might ruin harvests, but they did wonders for grassy pastures. Herds thrived and milk flowed. With a scarcity of bread people would turn to meat, cheese and butter, and keep the demand for the dairymen's produce high. Throughout the seventeenth century the supply of grain generally kept ahead of the needs of the rising population, and arable farmers complained about their paradoxical impoverishment through plenty. Dairy farmers, by contrast, were still in a seller's market.

The Yetminster farmers had one further thing to be grateful for. Their land lies on the geological formations of Jurassic rock. These provided two building stones, Cornbrash and Great Oolite. They were by no means the best for building, but the individual stones were good enough to be roughly shaped and laid horizontally in regular layers or courses. Some seams in the local quarries were better, and allowed the stone to be carved to form doorways, windows and copings.

So it came about that Yetminster farmers saw their profits rising in the later sixteenth and seventeenth centuries. Confident that these good times were going to continue and knowing that they could pass on both their land and their prosperity to succeeding generations, they set themselves to building and modernising their farmhouses.

The oldest stone house in Yetminster and for many miles around is Upbury Farm. Its blocked windows with their trefoiled heads are clearly medieval and suggest an original building date in the fifteenth century. The house was one of Yetminster's manor houses, perhaps built by one of the Salisbury clergy as a country house. From 1576 until 1729 the house and manor were leased to the Fitzjames family. It seems to have become no more than a grand farmhouse, providing younger sons of the family with a home and a small income. What we see now is the house they modernised. The old windows were blocked up, a chimney-stack was built to enclose the formerly open hearth, and a floor was thrown across the hall to make a house of two storeys from end to end. All this needed new glazed windows for the newly created rooms. More chimneys were added so that several rooms could have fireplaces, and they provided rather more comfort than in the old days.

This process of modernising houses happened not only at the top end of Yetminster's social scale, but also lower down among the yeomen, the nominal tenants of the manors. It can be seen most clearly at Spring Cottage in the outlying hamlet of Chetnole at the southern end of the old parish of Yetminster. It is not known who first built the house and who later modernised it, but one thing is clear: they were

Upbury Farm at Yetminster, the oldest and grandest house in this part of Dorset, which was probably built by one of the Salisbury clergy who owned the manor.

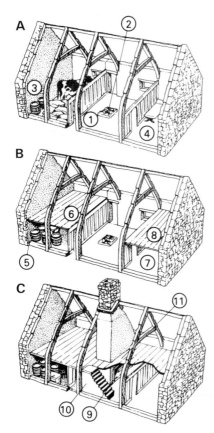

The three stages in the development of Spring Cottage. A: Hall (1) with open hearth (2), possible cow-house (3) and chamber (4). B: The cow-house has become a service room (5) and has been floored over (6) to provide more storage, and the chamber (7) has been similarly floored over (8). C: The transformation is complete with the provision of an enclosed hearth and chimney-stack (9) and stairs (10) up to a continuous upper floor (11).

not cottagers. The name of the house is recent, and a misnomer. Cottages were built for a particular, poor class of people who owned no land beyond the smallholding on which their homes stood. Spring Cottage was not one of these, but the house of a yeoman, a well-to-do farmer, who probably owned plenty of land. This was mostly pasture for a herd of milking cows that provided the wealth allowing him to build. In those days – the later Middle Ages – both land holdings and herds of cattle were small by our standards. A farm could prosper with a herd of only a dozen animals and 20 or 30 acres.

Although there are no documents for the house, its structure still tells part of the story. This starts not at ground level, but in the roof. Its timbers are all coated in soot. Although this could just possibly have been caused by a leaky chimney flue or an accidental fire, it is far more likely that it points to the origin of the house as an open hall. The soot came from the fire that once burned in its open hearth.

Some of the timbers are crucks. The great advantage of the cruck frame is that it is independent of both the walls and the roof, and supports them independently of each other. Here at Spring Cottage is evidence to suggest that the cruck frames originally supported timber-framed walls, not the stone ones that we presently see. These walls represent perhaps the last stage of rebuilding that gave Spring Cottage its modernised form.

The building started with an open hall at the centre, which contained the hearth. At one end there were two doors, one at the front and one at the back. This was the low end of the hall. At the high end was a partition dividing the hall from the chamber or private room, while another partition at the low end divided the hall from a further room. If cattle were kept there, Spring Cottage would have started as a long-house. Long-houses were often built in the western pastoral regions of England in the later Middle Ages, and Spring Cottage could have been one. It was modernised by stages, and the cattle were soon housed elsewhere. Perhaps the first stage was the substitution of the present heavy partition between the hall and the private chamber, though it may be an original feature. It is made of two kinds of vertical timber. These are heavy lengths of timber called 'muntins' with a groove each side and plain planks which slot into the grooves. They are secured top and bottom with horizontal timbers. These plank-and-muntin partitions are common in seventeenth-century houses in Dorset and the West Country. The earliest were being built at the end of the Middle Ages, and a late one in Herefordshire is carved with the date 1635. There are several plank-and-muntin partitions at Yetminster. Though none is dated, most appear to belong to the later sixteenth or early seventeenth century. These partitions often supported a series of joists that spanned the chamber and ceiled it – that is, formed a ceiling. The upper space created over the chamber provided extra storage. Much the same thing probably happened at the low end of the house.

In the next stage of modernisation the hall was given its enclosed hearth and chimney-stack. This allowed the hall to be entirely ceiled over. So Spring Cottage was lavishly fitted out with a fine box-panelled ceiling. The supporting beams were richly carved or moulded along their length to complement the plank-and-muntin partition. The house now had a continuous upper floor, end to end, reached by a staircase

The interior of the hall at Spring Cottage showing the inserted plank-and-muntin partition between the hall and the chamber beyond (incidentally still used as a sleeping room), and the panelled timber ceiling that was made possible when the open fire was enclosed by a chimney-stack.

adjacent to the chimney-stack. The final stage was the substitution of stone external walls for the original timber-framed ones, and it was given new windows filled with glass. The process of structural modernisation was then complete.

This plan, with three rooms in line and an internal chimney-stack forming one side of a cross passage between front and back entrances, evolved directly from the medieval arrangements with a central open hall. Houses with the same plan, either built from scratch or as the result of an evolving sequence of modernisations, were extremely popular in the later sixteenth and earlier seventeenth centuries. There are comparatively early new houses with this plan at Bloxham in Oxfordshire, built about 1550 if not before. From then onwards large numbers of these houses were built across the Cotswolds and down into Somerset, Dorset and Devon. In Yetminster the earliest dated house with this plan is Gable Court. It is now much altered, but date stones inscribed 1600 and 1601 show that the plan was used in the village at the start of the seventeenth century. By then it was probably already common, and it remained so until 1667, the date inscribed on what seems to be one of the last of these houses in Dorset.

We know nothing of the occupants of Spring Cottage or how they used their modernised house. However, Chetnole Farm, down the road, is a similar house, and it has an inventory in all probability belonging to it. This gives a fascinating picture of a rich yeoman farmer, Thomas Downton, who died in 1665. The details of his possessions allow us to make informed guesses about his life and household.

He was a rich man, worth £468 according to the inventory. Few other local yeoman farmers approached that sort of wealth. The documents suggest that their average wealth was only a fifth as great as his. It came from his land and his livestock, itemised in the inventory: 'Cattle in the ffeilds; Tenn Cowes & a bull, One steare & Two Two yeare age heaffers; ffoure Bulluckes' that were valued at £44 10s 0d, besides two mares and four colts at £12. The milk from the cattle

When a man died a detailed inventory was made of his belongings. (Sixteenth-century woodcut from a collection of ballads.)

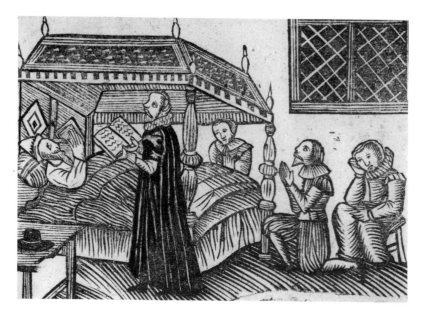

was used for cheese. A by-product of cheese-making is whey. This is not much use except as pig food, so Downton kept 'Tenn Cupples & fouteene hoggs; Two Piggs' (a pig in the seventeenth century was what today we would call a piglet). They added £11 to the value of the stock and no doubt provided the bacon for the house as well as a lot more for market.

To provide for the household bread and for winter fodder for the animals Downton kept 4½ acres of land for crops, and this gave him £10 worth of corn 'In the Barne' and 'wheate' and 'woats' in the fields.

The main living room in his farmhouse was still called the hall although it was floored over. It had a hearth, though this was not the only one in the house, and it was no longer open on all sides. It was contained within a very deep fire-place, which had a massive stone lintel with a niche carved out of the corner, perhaps to take a taper or candle to light the doorway into the hall. The inventory indeed mentions candlesticks, and it lists the fire-irons: 'Two andirons, a fire pan, a pair of tongs.' The furniture listed in the hall shows that it served as a dining-room: '1 tableboard, 1 cupboard and 1 chest, a livery board [the equivalent of a modern sideboard from where food could be served], six joined stools [finely joined by a furniture-maker, rather than roughly made with three legs pegged into a round seat], three cushions and a chair.' The chair no doubt was Downton's own and reflected the importance of his role as the head of the household. These contents are not so different from those of a medieval hall, though there are more of them and the room was more comfortable. There were cushions for the chairs, and the fire was no longer used for cooking.

Between the hall and the inner room there is a typical plank-and-muntin partition. The doorway through it has been enlarged by cutting curved sections out of the jambs. The explanation seems to be that this was to make it wide enough to allow barrels through, so the inner room was once not just a sleeping chamber, but a store room as well. It contained five barrels, but there were also some luxury items: linen worth £10, eighteen pieces of pewter worth £1 and a silver bowl and

The enclosed hearth at Chetnole Farm showing the massive stone lintel, which has a small niche carved out of its nearer corner to take a candlestick.

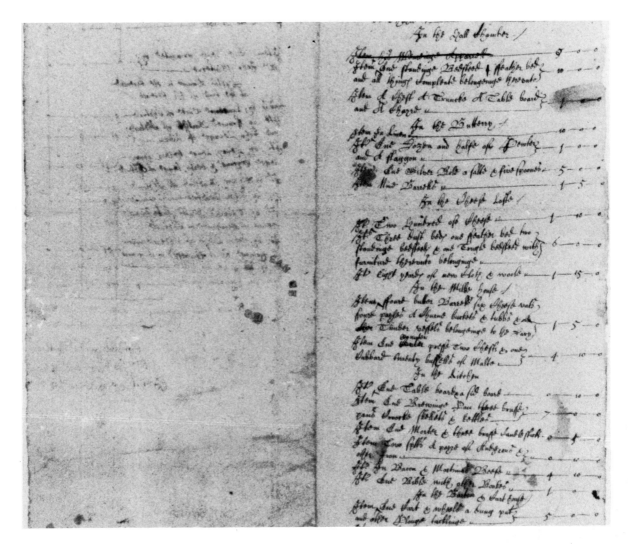

five spoons worth £5. Those figures for pewter and silver can be multiplied by well over a hundred to reach today's values. Here indeed are the luxury goods that so impressed Harrison.

Thomas Downton's inventory of 1665 listing his household possessions room by room, his farm stock, and his cash and debts.

The inventory includes a hall chamber with a feather bed and a bedstead and 'all things compleate belonginge thereunto' worth £10. It is not clear where this room was. It was still usual to sleep downstairs in the middle of the seventeenth century, but Thomas Downton and his wife could possibly have slept in the new room upstairs formed when the chimney-stack was inserted into the hall and it was ceiled over.

The hall is still clearly recognisable. So is the kitchen, though it seems to have been rebuilt after the inventory was made. It contained a table and a sideboard and many cooking utensils: one brewing pan, three brass pans, crocks, skillets and kettles; three brass candlesticks; two spits, a pair of andirons to hold them, and other iron. The only food mentioned was bacon and Martinmas beef. It must have been salted or smoked since it had to last for a feast. (Beef was expensive, even in pastoral areas like Yetminster, and reserved for special occasions.) The last items listed in the kitchen were perhaps intended to improve

A kitchen hearth enclosed by a brick stack at Selly Manor, Bournville, complete with bread oven, fire irons, pots, pans and utensils.

the shining hour while the food was cooking: 'One Bible and other Bookes, £1.' Some of Downton's household must therefore have been literate. This is not of itself surprising as wealthy men like Downton often could read and write. Nevertheless, literacy was not universal. One would like to know if his wife could also read and write and who else in the family could do so. Women were at a disadvantage educationally, and the poor were formally instructed in little beyond religious doctrine in the form of the Catechism. This taught acceptance of the social order and obedience to one's master as well as instilling common morality and Christian precepts. Few taught the rural poor to read and write until the nineteenth century.

Somewhere at the back of the house was the main workroom, the milk house or dairy. It was filled with four butter barrels, six cheese vats, four pails, a churn, buckets and tubs, and all the other vessels needed in a dairy for making butter and cheese. Upstairs was a room called the 'cheese loft', though it was more than that suggests. Here two hundred cheeses were stored, and they were worth £1 10s. There were also 8 yards of new cloth and some wool worth nearly as much. It would be interesting to know if the Downtons were part-time weavers as well as dairy farmers. This was often the case in the West Country, but there is no mention of a spinning-wheel or loom in the inventory.

The cheese loft had a further use beyond storage. It was a bedroom. In it were three 'dust beds' and one 'ffeather bed' and they were almost certainly for the household, the children and servants who helped on the farm and in the dairy. They also slept together. Children and servants never had any privacy. Because they had to go upstairs to sleep Downton could check that they were all present before he himself retired.

Finally, the inventory shows that Downton was a capitalist and played an important economic role in the village. Like other yeomen he had plenty of capital invested in his stock and in his household, £152 in all, if the inventory was complete. But he was also worth a further £316, a sum made up of ten debts owing to him. Two were expressly mentioned as mortgages, the others simply as debts, mostly to local people. In an age without banks, he was financing other people's enterprises by granting mortgages to other farmers, to buy land perhaps, and to build houses, and by making other loans to help local people who were suddenly pressed for ready cash. Time and again inventories around the country list these debts. Occasionally there were mistakes, and money was lent to people who could not or would not repay, and the inventories point them out as desperate debts. Downton seems to have been lucky. There were no desperate debts in his inventory.

As the seventeenth century progressed there was a major change in the layout of rooms. The arrangement of early houses like Spring Cottage and Chetnole Farm with vestiges of the old medieval hall in the centre became obsolete. The chimney-stack that took up so much internal space in the central hall was moved to an external wall. Usually there were two stacks, one on each gable wall at the ends of the house. That saved building materials and labour as well. The entrance to the house could still be in the middle, but now it opened into a vestibule that led to a room either side, the kitchen and the parlour, and to the staircase. We call this vestibule the hall or staircase hall, but it has nothing to do with the old medieval hall in these yeoman houses. It had the great advantage of providing circulation space. This made the individual rooms more private because, instead of one room leading off another, they all had separate access from the vestibule. As the idea of circulation space developed, you could get more and more privacy. Eventually master and servants could have separate quarters, and bedrooms could be entirely private; instead of one leading off another, all could have separate entrances from a landing.

The functions of the old hall were now split. Cooking and eating took place in the room on one side of the entrance, now called the kitchen. The formal functions of the hall now took place in the room on the other side of the entrance vestibule, the parlour. For a while the parlour remained a best bedroom, but it was also a room where formal meals could be eaten away from the servants and where guests could be politely entertained. There were always subsidiary rooms, and often these were built at the back rather than at the ends.

By the early eighteenth century, the beds were all generally upstairs. The upper storey too was divided into rooms, a best bedroom over the parlour for the head of the house and his wife, and further bedrooms over the kitchen and service rooms for the rest of the household. These upstairs rooms would still have to double as store rooms, though there might be lofts in the roof space overhead.

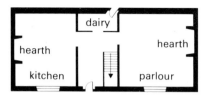

The later yeoman houses in Yetminster had their hearths on the gabled end walls, one for the kitchen and one for the parlour. This left space for an entrance vestibule and staircase in the middle of the house, and a cool dairy either at the rear (as shown) or beside the entrance.

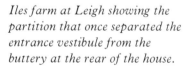

Iles farm at Leigh showing the partition that once separated the entrance vestibule from the buttery at the rear of the house.

Such houses with central entrance vestibules and chimneys on the gable walls began to appear in large numbers after the middle of the seventeenth century. Nevertheless, there are earlier examples. In Yetminster the earliest dated house with this form is Higher Farm, which has date stones inscribed 'AW 1624' and 'AW 1630'. Iles Farm at Leigh is possibly earlier. Bob Machin believes that it was built about 1590–1600, remarkably early. If this is correct, it may be because it was built by a member of the gentry, showing once more how a fashion descended down the ranks of society. An inventory of 1677 shows the parlour at one end of Iles Farm. It still contained beds, and a table with a carpet over it, the predecessor of our tablecloths. Then there were stools and chairs, as well as chests, boxes and a trunk that were used to store linen and clothes. At the other end of the house was the hall, again with a table and carpet, a bench and chairs. Interestingly, there was a clock worth 30s. This may have been one of the new pendulum clocks that started to appear in the later seventeenth century and at last brought a reasonably accurate timepiece to the home.

The best decorative feature to survive inside Iles Farm is the partition between the entrance vestibule and the buttery at the rear. Characteristically, it is made of planks and muntins. In the centre is a doorway, and over the top is an open balustrade to admit light and air through to the rear service room.

Service rooms containing food and drink had to be kept cool, so if they had windows they were best shaded. Sometimes they were fitted with louvres (horizontal wooden slats) to keep out the sun, sometimes they simply faced north. A cool room was always essential for a dairy. To make butter, milk has to be allowed to stand in a shallow pan overnight, preferably at a temperature of about 55 degrees Fahrenheit (13 degrees Celsius). In many parts of the country, especially in the north and west, diaries were built in the north or north-east corners of houses. Here at Yetminster they were often placed in the centre. The middle of the house was no longer heated because the hearths

were at the ends, so a dairy placed in the centre could be kept cool, and if it were near the entrance it could be airy as well. A balustraded opening like the one at Iles Farm or a simpler open louvre allowed a draught of cooling air into the dairy. Stone floors and shelves helped to maintain a fairly uniform cool temperature. There is a fine, completely fitted-out dairy like this at Manor Farm, placed in the centre of the house beside the entrance and between the parlour and kitchen. It has a small window, high up on the west wall, but it rarely gets the sun and the room stays cool even in midsummer. On one side is a built-in, shallow, lead pan in the form of a tray or upturned lid. Milk was poured into it and left overnight to allow the cream to rise to the surface. It was then skimmed off and poured into a butterchurn, and churned by hand for a few minutes. The butter was removed and patted into shape and pressed with a symbol, the mark of the farm, before being sent to market. The skimmed milk was turned into cheese. It was curdled and then pressed into a mould to squeeze out all the whey. The whey went back to the farmyard to feed the pigs.

All this was women's work. While the men were busy in the fields and at market, the women milked the cows, brought the milk to the dairy, churned the butter and pressed the cheese. They also had work to do in the orchards and the fields. Altogether they played a crucial role in the economic success of the farm. On top of this they ran the household, bore the babies and succoured the children who survived. This life was age-old by the seventeenth century, but it is only then that there is enough documentary evidence to throw a vivid light on the details of household life.

The dairy at Manor Farm, Yetminster, still fitted out with shelves, a large rectangular lead pan used in skimming the milk (on the right) and some of the implements used in butter-making. The small window helps to ventilate the room and keep it cool without letting in too much direct sunlight.

Milking time in the fields – a woman at work in the seventeenth century. (Seventeenth-century woodcut from a collection of ballads.)

Men on average did not marry until their late twenties, women until their mid-twenties. Even these late marriages took place possibly earlier in life than was the case two centuries before in the later Middle Ages. That may be a reason for the rising population of the sixteenth and seventeenth centuries, and its greater resilience to the effects of plague and infectious disease. A newly married couple would start to have children at once, but low fertility and, apparently, even the practice of some form of contraception in the seventeenth century limited marriages on average to eight pregnancies, though at least double this number was theoretically possible. One child in five was likely to die before a year was out, and at least one more would never reach maturity. Death culled the whole population, not just the aged, so it is no wonder that the population grew only slowly. This had two consequences for the household. It seldom contained more than two generations – few lived long enough to see their grandchildren – and a large part of every village's population was children, perhaps even 40 per cent. This happy picture has its grim side.

Disease picked off the children, and they succumbed with terrible regularity. Because of this, some historians have argued that parents thought of their children as expendable and gave them little emotional affection. Nevertheless, there is definite evidence to show that childhood was not a harsh period of lamentable neglect and abuse, to be endured as best you could. It was certainly a time of hard work. There were small farmyard tasks for children from the age of four. They were set to scare off the crows from newly sown cornfields. They helped their mothers with gleaning for fallen grain after harvest. There were animals to be tended and fed. But there was plenty of affection, and grief overflowed at the continual untimely deaths, such as that of John Martindale, the young son of a Chester yeoman, whose early death so 'distracted' his parents, as his father recorded, that it brought their lives to a standstill while they consoled each other.

Between a third and a quarter of children lived in households where death had taken a mother or father. It is no coincidence that fairy tales abound with stories of the cruelty of wicked stepparents. Yet a household needed a husband and a housewife if it were to function efficiently. If one died early, another must be found to fill the vacant place.

Women were just as important as men as far as work was concerned. The dairies of Yetminster make that abundantly clear. But in the eyes of the law women were certainly not *equal* to men. The parish records show the superior status of men. Nearly always they owned the property. They ran society. While only the priesthood was actually forbidden to women, they nevertheless deferred to their menfolk in everything, at least so far as the law was concerned. This gave a husband the legal right of ownership of his household, even though his wife ran it. A housewife could usually gain legal possession of the house only when the male line failed. During the Civil War of the 1640s some women briefly became masters of their households when their men were away fighting, but the Restoration took away whatever privilege they had gained. Yet, though women were at a disadvantage before the law, though they were economically exploited, socially inferior and often uneducated, they did overcome these disadvantages. During a period when Elizabeth, Mary and Anne rose to queenhood, even ordinary

A narrow lane near Yetminster, with a lonely cottage built on the waste land between the roadway and a hedge marking the boundary of the fields.

women of unusual character, persistence or fortune could rise to commanding positions in society or wield strong influence in local family life.

Wealth and leisure certainly increased in the seventeenth century, but not for the majority. Life for landless labourers was one continuous struggle. They might fall ill or simply be unable to cope. Their labours might be spurned by changes in the market. Ruin could soon overtake them. The laws of economics were to ruin many of them in the eighteenth century, when agricultural success brought first plenty, then falling prices and finally recession. By that time you could not afford to pay a labourer much, if you could afford him at all.

Labourers who married and set up house independently were the true cottagers, a legal term of medieval origin. The houses of these poor people seldom survive. Here and there around Yetminster are stone houses, like Honeycombe Cottage in Thornford Lane, that began with two rooms, one up and one down, but these were the best of the houses of the landless. Most of their cottages were flimsy structures made of mud with roughly thatched roofs. They crowded into the gaps between the grand, stone houses. They rose on any strips of land taken from the verges of the road, and indeed several later cottages, mostly of the nineteenth century, survive like this in the lanes around Yetminster to remind us of the poor.

The poor were always there. Like the children, they filled the villages in a way we cannot easily visualise today. This is clear from the remarkable population tables drawn up by Gregory King in the 1690s, which he called the *Scheme of the income and expense of the several families of England*. He numbered the population at $5\frac{1}{2}$ million. Of this, half comprised people who, in King's terminology, increased the national wealth. They included Yetminster's yeomanry and everyone higher on the social ladder up to the aristocracy. The other half were the poor who, despite their labours, King said were decreasing the nation's wealth. A few were soldiers and sailors. The bulk were evenly split among either labourers and servants or cottagers and paupers. There were nearly 3 million of them. We cannot be precise about King's meaning nor sure of the accuracy of his figures, but his general conclusion is unmistakable. About half the population at best could just manage to feed, clothe and house itself, at worst could do none of these things. At best they crowded into Yetminster's long-vanished cottages, eking out meagre wages by what they could grow in their yards. At worst they lived off the poor rate in cottages rented for them, wearing cast-off clothes and spending the few pennies allowed them to fill empty bellies.

Even they had one advantage. They were the poor who belonged to Yetminster because they were born there. Under the Elizabethan poor law no parish was responsible for other people's poor. Those who did not belong were sent packing, unless someone with Christian charity called everyone his brother. But even those with kind hearts had to be careful – one charitable act might attract an endless clamour for more. Always there were the utterly destitute, cast off and belonging nowhere. Like the bubonic plague until 1666, like pneumonia, like smallpox, influenza and typhus, poverty was a chronic disease. Its victims were daily found dead in ditches, or huddled under the straw in a corner of the barn. These were their last homes.

Always the poor must be set beside the grand, stone yeoman houses that make the Yetminster of today. It is right that they should cast a

A particularly grand plank-and-muntin partition and panelled ceiling at Manor House, Yetminster.

shadow over a sunny picture-postcard view of Merrie England. It is not right, though, that they should dispel it. England had been poorer in the Middle Ages. All but a handful of people came face to face with starvation then. Invasion, insurrection, disease and plague gave death a triumphant image. By the seventeenth century, people had cause for optimism. Half the population led fruitful lives. Half the population saw their old age. Our Yetminster and many villages like it were built by these people. If you had reached the level in society that Gregory King believed was increasing the nation's wealth, you should count yourself lucky. And indeed England's yeomanry by and large did recognise its good fortune.

In 1642 Thomas Fuller, once the rector of Broadwindsor in Dorset, wrote an essay called *The holy state and the profane state*. In it he eulogised the good yeoman 'living in the temperate zone betwixt greatness and want; an estate of people almost peculiar to England. France and Italy are like a die, which hath no points between cinque and ace, – nobility and peasantry'. The pamphleteer John Aylmer took the superiority of England's yeomanry much further, especially when he compared them with the downtrodden German (Almane) equivalent.

> They eate hearbes and thou Beefe and Mutton. Thei rotes: and thou butter, chese and egges. Thei drinck commonly water: and thou good ale and beare. . . . Thou wouldst vii times of the day fall flat on they face before God, and geve him thanks, that thou was born an English man, and not a french pezant, nor an Italyan, nor Almane.

This was perhaps true of Yetminster's yeomen, but the landlords of neighbouring manors never allowed their peasantry to progress so far, and in the eighteenth century were willing to inflict real hardship on their villagers in the course of self-aggrandisement. But Yetminster was not alone. Hundreds of villages could tell a similar story. It would never be exactly the same. Different crops, other animals, changes in landholding, timber or brick rather than good building stone, new faces above all make each story unique. Without documents some will only be half told. Lose the buildings as well and the stories are gone forever. So Yetminster has a special place in the history of the seventeenth century. It was a microcosm of half of England.

CHAPTER THREE
The Industrious Home

Everywhere in Dobcross there are houses with unusually long bands of windows. This was a weaving village, and the windows lit the looms where handweavers used to work over their living-rooms. Dobcross is one of several villages that make up the ancient township of Saddleworth on the western edge of the Pennines. Like all these villages Dobcross is silent now, and has been for generations. But once it was full of noise, the clumping of packhorses as they brought in supplies of wool and took away finished pieces of broadcloth to market, the clatter of clogs as people went about their work, and, over all, the heavy clacking and thumping of looms.

Until even a hundred years ago it was common in England for the house to be a workplace as well as a home in the modern sense. All kinds of industries have been sheltered within our houses; metal-working, pottery and basket-making are some of the more ancient ones. None has so intimate a connection with the home than weaving. Our ancestors in the second millennium BC spun wool into yarn and wove it into cloth in their homes and then sent it to market. The last handweavers were still at work in very different homes at the beginning of this century, eighty years ago. At the end of the eighteenth century weaving in the home reached the height of its prosperity. On the Pennines of the West Riding of Yorkshire between Oldham and Huddersfield hardly a place was untouched by it, and hundreds and hundreds of houses were newly built or adapted to contain rooms on the upper floors to serve as loomshops or weaving lofts. They are all marked by long bands of windows to let in the maximum daylight to illuminate the looms, the spinning jennies and all the other equipment needed to make thousands of pieces of cloth every year.

Weaving started as a cottage industry in the Pennines towards the end of the Middle Ages as a consequence of a long series of changes in land use. In 1069–1070 William the Conqueror devastated the North to ensure its submission to his rule, and much of the Pennines then came into the hands of the monastic orders, especially the newly founded Cistercians who began to recolonise the land. They herded vast flocks of sheep on the moors, sold the wool to Flemish and Italian weavers and spent the profits on their glorious abbeys. Fountains, Rievaulx and Roche were among them. Some of the Saddleworth hills indeed belonged to Roche Abbey, and its sheep helped to pay for the building of the abbey church in the 1170s.

Economic decline and the Black Death of 1348–1350 changed all that. Labour became expensive and the land cheap, upsetting and often ruining the great landowners, but encouraging the surviving peasantry. On the Pennines the great monastic houses progressively retired from farming and leased out their land for longer and longer terms to peasant yeomen.

The Pennine landscape above Delph with enclosed fields in the foreground and middle distance, remnants of a tree-choked valley in between, and the open moorland beyond.

The new yeomen leaseholders soon established customary rights to their land and changed the system of farming. They grew a little corn – mostly oats – for their own household consumption and to feed their cattle in winter, and made good profits from cattle-rearing and dairying on farms called vaccaries, with cheese as their major marketable produce. Many of the names of their early settlements reflect this new economy. The suffix 'stall', as in Heptonstall and Rawtenstall, and the prefix 'booth' in Boothroyd and Boothstead indicate where cattle were stalled, and the suffix 'royd' in Mytholmroyd and Ibbotsroyd indicates a clearing in the woodland for one of these settlements. Although life was hard, there were benefits not found in the more prosperous grain-growing counties of the Midlands. In wet years, when the local harvest failed but the pastures filled with grass, there was enough profit from dairying to buy grain to feed the family and supplement the hay as winter fodder for the animals. Moreover, life was not the endless drudgery needed by arable fields, where every day of the year was occupied by some task from ploughing through to threshing and winnowing the corn. The cattle, of course, needed to be tended. They needed to be milked during the summer months and fed during the winter. The cheese had to be made. The small fields needed attention the year round. But there was time to spare. Weaving was a profitable way of making use of this spare time and was increasingly taken up. By the seventeenth century, it was becoming more and more important as a source of income because of the nature of land tenure. These farmers practised a form of partible inheritance whereby their land on the flanks of the hills was divided at death among their children. The origins of partible inheritance are ancient and obscure, but it was commonly practised in the pastoral areas of the country, in Kent, Essex and East Anglia, in the West Country and Wales, and in much of the North. It was an equable system, discouraging the accumulation of wealth in a few hands and, in theory at least, giving everyone a start in life on which they could build if they were enterprising.

While the population remained fairly static, the average size of landholdings did not decline as a result of partible inheritance. There was in any case plenty of land for the sparse number of people here. The high open moors were commons that everyone could use as summer pasture, and there was still land to colonise down in the steep, tree-choked valleys with their rushing streams. But this prospect of land for all attracted new colonists, and as the population grew from the sixteenth century onwards it eventually brought the land under pressure. Its poor fertility and the harsh climate affected corn first: there was not enough arable land to go round. Then, with the constant division and subdivision of landholdings caused by partible inheritance and the growing numbers of people, the size of individual landholdings began to decline and families could no longer make enough profit from dairying to buy grain to feed themselves and their cattle in winter. With time on their hands they increasingly turned to cottage industry, weaving here at Saddleworth, and in other parts of the Pennines stocking-knitting, quarrying, coal-mining, lead-mining and smelting. 'The tenants are much increased in number more than they were,' explained a witness to a court dispute in 1643,

> and the tenements become so small in quantity that many of them are not above three or four acres apiece and generally not above nine acres so that they could not maintain their families were it not by their industry.

The earliest surviving houses found on the Pennines in any number date from this time. Around Saddleworth they are fairly small, with little more than the two ground-floor rooms and a loft that can be seen in a farmhouse called Windy Nook at Grotton, a hamlet in the west of the township.

The north side of Windy Nook at Saddleworth. When new in 1648 the only opening was the doorway on the right with the heavy lintel, which is carved with the date and Henry Shaw's initials.

In the Middle Ages commercial weaving on a national level had become concentrated in towns like York and Beverley in the North, and, in the South, Salisbury and Marlborough in Wiltshire. It was generally on a small scale. This was a time when much of Britain's wool was exported to Italy and the Low Countries, and finished cloth was imported. In the middle of the fourteenth century this state of affairs began to change. A major cause was the Hundred Years' War with France, which disrupted imports of cloth; also the Crown imposed heavy duties on the export of wool, so the nascent weaving industry was encouraged in many parts of the country.

Weaving did not necessarily flourish only where there were the largest flocks of sheep. Sheep were commonly herded where arable farming was also practised, and there were strong manorial controls and little spare labour for anything beyond the needs of the fields. Sheep were valued as much for the manure they gave the fields as for their wool or meat. In dairying and cattle-rearing country, however, manorial control was often weak and the land was in the hands of either freeholders or those with secure tenure, as on the Pennines and, too, at Yetminster. People had more spare time and could use it as they wished. There was another reason. Unlike sheep, cattle need plenty of water to drink, and water is also essential in weaving. Indeed, the industry's first need was for a good supply of clear, soft water for the various stages of washing the wool, preparing the yarn and finishing the cloth. This included fulling the woven cloth, a process whereby the fibres are felted together by being beaten with wooden hammers. Already in the Middle Ages water mills had been adapted to power the fulling hammers, so water had the double function of being indispensable to the finishing process as well as providing the power for it. So weaving became concentrated in places where dairying and cattle farming were already established, such as the Weald of Kent, part of Essex and Suffolk, and the West Country. On the Pennines it was slow to start, but here the industry eventually flourished the most strongly and left its imprint on the landscape the most clearly.

Not only did weaving provide a household with a way out of an economic predicament, but it was also easy to set up in business. All the family could join in. At the end of the seventeenth century a spinning-wheel cost only 1s and a loom about 15s, while a cow cost £2 16s, between three and four times as much, and an ox cost over £4. Although some wool came from local sheep, even the farmer's own, the bulk came from elsewhere, as Daniel Defoe recounted in *The Complete English Tradesman*:

> The rest of the Leicestershire wool merchants, who do not bring their wool southward, carry it forward to the north, to Wakefield, Leeds, and Halifax; here they mix it with, and use it among northern wool, which is not esteemed so fine . . . notwithstanding that they have a great deal of very fine wool from . . . the wolds or downs in the East Riding of Yorkshire, and from the bishoprick of Durham, more especially the banks of the Tees, where . . . the grounds are rich and the sheep thought to be the largest in England.

The wool had to be bought at markets like Halifax and Huddersfield from wool merchants called 'staplers', or occasionally from the larger

A seventeenth-century window at New Tame with chamfered mullions and carved hood-mould.

sheep farmers. It was then taken to the weaver's farm on a packhorse, though someone weaving on the largest scale might buy a year's supply of wool in bulk direct from the sheep farmer. While much capital was invested in the weaving industry in many parts of the country, on the Pennines weaving remained a family affair for a long time. It was financed within the family, and the whole process of turning wool into cloth was undertaken by the family as well.

Because of the harsh climate and the inhospitable terrain, it was not until well after the Middle Ages that Pennine yeomen generally achieved enough wealth to start building substantial houses. Only during the seventeenth century did they at last begin to use stone for their houses quite commonly. This had already been happening in the South for some time, at Yetminster and in hundreds of other southern and Midland villages where good stone could be quarried. It was an overt demonstration of increasing wealth. Stone was easily quarried or delved from the Pennine hillsides, and the name of one of the Saddleworth villages, Delph, may originate in just such a quarry. The quarries produced hard, carboniferous stones, either Coal Measures or, as around Saddleworth, Millstone Grit. It is hard-wearing and tough, and able to withstand both rough weather and the mason's chisel, so decorative carving was expensive and usually kept to a minimum. There might be a decorated doorway with a date stone and plain, chamfered window openings, and sometimes an overhanging hood-mould with decorated ends designed to throw off rainwater, but little else.

Because of the strength of the stone, the upright mullions between the individual lights of the windows were strong enough to carry the whole weight of the lintels that spanned them, however long they were, and all the masonry above that. Long windows were highly beneficial, as the Pennines are a notably gloomy part of the country and daylight is precious. Moreover, in the early days of building in stone, a long window, because it was expensive to carve and fit out with glass, was a mark of status that would reflect the importance of the principal room inside.

As in Yetminster, the larger houses followed the old medieval pattern with three rooms in a line. In the middle was the principal room, a hall, which in the North was called the 'firehouse' because it contained the only fire, or simply the 'house' or 'housepart' as it was the principal room and used for living, cooking and dining. Next to it were a service room at one end and a private room at the other. Yeomen with less money to spend – and they were in the majority on the wetter, western flanks of the Pennines – commonly built smaller houses of only two rooms, a firehouse and an inner room that combined the functions of service and private room and was used for sleeping and for storing and preparing food. A light partition might subdivide the room to separate the two functions. In early houses like Windy Nook the division between the firehouse and the inner room was a stout, timber-framed partition. This was the northern equivalent of the plank-and-muntin partitions of the West Country. They were later made of stone. Again, in early houses there was a loft used for storage and perhaps as a bedroom for children and servants. It was reached by a ladder-stair from the inner room. In many early houses the smoke from the fire in the housepart was confined by a hood built on the inside of the gable wall. The hood was of timber and lined with plaster to make it fireproof. It projected several feet from the wall and rested on a strong beam across the firehouse at ceiling height. The space beneath it formed an ingle where the family could sit to keep warm. One side of the ingle was an external wall with a small window known as a fire-window to light the ingle. The other side of the ingle would stop short of the opposite external wall at a partition or 'heck', to use the northern word. The heck kept out the draught, as the main entrance to the house would be just beyond

A view looking into an early Pennine house such as Windy Nook. The ingle (1) is warmed by a fire on a hearth (2) backing the end wall. It is protected from draughts from the front door by a heck (3), while the smoke is carried away by a timber and plaster hood (4). The ingle has its own 'fire-window' (5).

it, perhaps in the gable wall, perhaps in the front wall. The North had no use for entrance vestibules and passages that led to separate rooms as had begun to appear at Yetminster in the seventeenth century.

Later houses had stone flues, but often the ingle with its fire-window and heck remained. Instead of lofts there were now full upper storeys divided into chambers for sleeping. The one over the firehouse would be for the master and his wife, and it might have a hearth and fire-window of its own. The inner room downstairs now became a service room, perhaps with a cellar beneath it, and, because most people were dairy farmers, a dairy might be partitioned from it. Both would again have chambers over them to provide a second and third bedroom for the family and servants.

Windy Nook, the earliest known house of this type to be securely dated, has a date stone over the entrance marked '1648 HS'. It records that the house was built by Henry Shaw, one of the first generation of yeoman farmers in the locality to build in stone. Opposite the timber-framed partition between the firehouse and inner room there was originally a timber hood over the fire, but it has been replaced by the present enclosed hearth with a stone chimney-stack. The ingle is marked by a pair of fire-windows on the south side of the house, and the firehouse originally had a window of four lights. Apart from the entrance that opened on to the heck, the north side of the house is bare, with only a later, modern window for the inner room. Some houses, especially those built on a south-facing slope, had no windows at all on the north simply to keep out the piercing winter weather.

Most of these two-roomed stone yeoman houses were built in the later seventeenth and early eighteenth centuries. By then they were very old-fashioned by the standards of Yetminster and the south of the country. Many carry a date stone, a sign of their builders' pride. Saddleworth Fold is dated 1699, the ruinous Boothstead at Denshaw 1724, and there are many more. They were no doubt once the commonest houses around Saddleworth, but demolition, alteration and enlargement have made examples in anything like their original state fairly rare. These changes were often brought about by the expansion of the weaving industry in the home as it became more extensive and profitable. At first spinning and weaving were done wherever they might fit into these houses. None of the implements was particularly large or heavy, and they could all be put away after use. Either rooms were adapted for the purpose, or small sheds were constructed against each house. First the wool was prepared for spinning by washing it. Then it was carded by drawing it between two boards or cards set with wire, like a pair of brushes, so as to align the fibres before spinning. Even children could do this, and like everyone else they were kept occupied in busy households. Traditionally women did the lighter work of spinning, giving us the term 'spinster'. Originally they spun wool on a distaff, a spindle with a weight attached to it. By rapidly spinning it, a woman could twist carded wool into a length of yarn, twist in another length and so on until the yarn was long. The spinning-wheel made the process much quicker, and a foot treadle to operate the wheel freed her hands for the continuous feeding in of the carded wool. To make the wool weave more easily, hanks or bobbins of yarn were wetted and spun until damp-dry by whirling or 'wuzzing' them

Wuzzing-holes at Diggle.

Tenter posts on the hills above Delph, showing the notches that carried the tenter-frame. In the middle distance to the right are the enclosed fields where cattle were pastured and small crops of oats grown.

round in a basket slung from a stick. One end of the stick was inserted into a hole called a 'wuzzing hole' drilled in a convenient stone, either on the side of a house or in a field wall. These odd little holes can be seen wherever there used to be weavers at work.

The first small looms were used to weave kersey, a narrow coarse cloth made from short-fibred or short-staple wool that may take its name from the Suffolk weaving village of Kersey. The woven cloth was sent away to a local mill to be fulled and then came back perhaps to be dyed and to be given a final wash. It was then stretched on hooks set in a frame known as a 'tenter' to dry without shrinking or warping. This is where the phrase 'on tenterhooks' comes from. The frames were fixed to rows of posts about 6 to 8 feet high and about the same distance apart. Most were of wood and have now vanished, but stone tenter posts have survived. There is a fine row of eleven posts and remains of four more at Wall Hill above Dobcross. They were erected in the 1840s, and must have been one of the last tenters to go up out of doors before the process of drying was moved inside to avoid the change-able Pennine weather.

The wool industry developed quickly. By the start of the eighteenth century a third of the Yorkshiremen of the West Riding, according to their wills, were principally occupied in the wool industry. It was then that Daniel Defoe, in his account of *A Tour thro' the Whole Island of Great Britain*, described the industry in the Pennines some way to the north-east of Saddleworth. Riding along the ancient Roman trackway over Blackstone Edge to Halifax, he came first upon a few houses, and then more and more as he descended the moors:

> houses scattered and spread upon the sides of the hills even from the top to the bottom . . . hardly a house standing out of speaking distance from another.

Each had a few small enclosures of land belonging to it, though not more than a few acres. Every clothier, Defoe noted, kept a horse, perhaps two, to fetch and carry wool or cloth. There were a few cows in the enclosures as well, though 'they scarce sow corn enough for their cocks and hens'. Clearly some farmer–clothiers were less dependent on farming than they had been.

> Almost at every house was a tenter, look which way we would, it was all the same, innumerable houses and tenters . . . and almost on every tenter a piece of cloth or kersie . . . from which the sun glancing (the white reflecting its rays) to us, I thought it was the most agreeable sight that I ever saw.

Beside each house was a rill of running water and 'every house was a work-house with the water running into and through it' to be used in the various processes of cloth-making. Strangely, there were no people about. Then Defoe discovered why. They were all indoors weaving.

> If we knocked at the door of any of the master manufacturers, we presently saw a house full of lusty fellows, some at the dye-vat, some dressing the cloths, some in the loom, all hard at work, and full employed.

It was not just the men who were working, either. Women were busy spinning, and even the children were carding the wool before passing it on to their mothers and elder sisters: 'Scarce any thing above four years old but its hands were sufficient for its own support.'

In Saddleworth there was a similar concentration on weaving. In Defoe's time, the 1720s, even as many as three-quarters of Saddleworth families were engaged in this industry. Before the end of the eighteenth century farming was a secondary pursuit and nine families out of ten were in weaving. The population was then growing at an unprecedented rate. The reason for this increase is unclear, but it may be that people were less dependent on the land for wealth, because as weavers they could set up as householders at an earlier age than they usually could if they had to wait for an inheritance of land. That meant earlier marriages, a longer child-bearing span for the women and so an increased birth-rate. On top of this, the greater wealth of the yeoman class brought an improvement in housing and probably better nutrition. These factors may have helped to reduce mortality, but unfortunately statistics are scarce and inconclusive, and do not resolve this question.

Various technological developments in the eighteenth century made looms more efficient and so benefited the weavers. In 1733 John Kay patented the fly-shuttle, a mechanical means of passing the yarn that formed the weft (horizontal or crossways threads) from one side of the warp (vertical or longways threads) to the other. It slowly replaced the laborious method of doing it by hand. However, a loom with a fly-shuttle could be operated by a single weaver without an assistant, and consequently its introduction evoked angry opposition from some weavers who saw their jobs threatened. Yet within twenty years the innovation was being accepted, and by the end of the century it was in widespread use. The fly-shuttle and the development of larger and heavier looms meant that weavers could produce wider cloth called 'broadcloth'. By 1780 this had taken the place of the narrow kersey as the principal product of areas such as Saddleworth. The spinners were by now under constant pressure to keep a single weaver in yarn. The demand for cloth was insatiable, the profits good, and weavers were not troubled by unemployment.

Weaving windows at High Kinders, Saddleworth. The top band have their original small leaded panes and an opening sash window in the centre to adjust the temperature inside.

The loomshop in the museum at Spring Bank, Golcar.

To accommodate the new large looms, purpose-built rooms were needed. They had to be large with plenty of headroom, as well as airy, light and clean. They also had to be dry and warm, as wool is best woven in a warm, dry atmosphere. The best and most economical way to achieve this was to adapt the upper storey of one's house, perhaps by raising the walls and roof a little, and by extending the windows from the customary four or five lights until they were double the length and more, and they stretched in a band from one side to the other, front and back. In this way a large, light room was provided. It was cheaper

A stretch of watershot masonry in Dobcross.

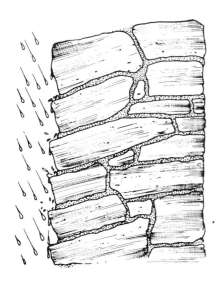

A section of watershot masonry with the outer face of the wall on the left, the inner face on the right, showing in exaggerated form how the outer courses of masonry slope downhill and form ledges. The aim is to reduce the penetration of water into the mortar.

to do this than to build afresh with new foundations, and the tough Pennine stone could easily support more storeys. The stone mullions too, even when dividing a very long window, were quite adequate to bear the weight of more walling and a roof over them.

Another advantage was that these windows were not highly rated for the onerous tax that the government levied on windows from 1696 until 1851. Although the band might contain a dozen lights – and at least once a band of twenty was built – for the purpose of the tax they counted as a single window because the width of the mullions was less than half the specified 12-inch limit above which the lights would have counted as separate windows.

An innovation in house-building of the later eighteenth century that seems to have been brought southwards from Cumbria was the use of watershot masonry. This involved laying the outward-facing courses of stone so that they sloped gently downwards, apparently to deter the driving rain from penetrating into the mortar. This helped to keep the weaving lofts dry. The need for dry rooms was another reason for building upwards. In an age without damp-proof courses, ground-floor rooms were prone to damp, whereas an upstairs room could be kept dry and always received a little warmth from the living-rooms below. Often a small fireplace was provided in the weaving room to maintain the required temperature throughout the year. This was further controlled because a few of the individual window lights could be opened.

Many houses were adapted to provide weaving lofts in this way. Oakwood at Diggle on the Saddleworth hills was first built by the Rhodes family about 1740 as an ordinary farmhouse like Windy Nook, but later it had its upper storey raised and was given a band of eleven windows to light the new, large broadcloth looms that had been installed.

An inventory of a Honley weaver who died in 1775 shows how these two-roomed farmhouses with a weaving room in the upper storey were used. The main living-room served as a kitchen and dining-room and was called the 'house'. It contained irons, pots and pans for cooking, and tables and chairs. The inner room, in this document called by the southern word 'parlour', was a bedroom as well as a private room and had the best bed, a table and chairs, and a 'large bibell'. The upper storey was divided into a great chamber that was used for carding and spinning, and a little chamber that was the loomshop. Outside the house there was a tenter-ground for drying finished pieces of cloth.

Another similar house, again close to the start of the open moors, where adaptation was more extensive, is Pinfold Farm. A yeoman farmer called Edmund Buckley was living here in 1662 when it was a typical two-roomed farmhouse with a loft over it. Its name indeed means 'an enclosure for cattle'. But the Buckleys soon took up weaving and became clothiers as well as farmers. In the 1750s they built a weaving loft into the upper storey and gave it a window of six lights. Later still they rebuilt and extended the house at the parlour end by adding a slaughterhouse to it. Inside the slaughterhouse, the chain for tethering the doomed animal is still to be seen, and so is the slab of stone on which its carcass was butchered. Above the slaughterhouse they placed a taking-in door to enable bales of wool carried up to the farm by packhorses to be brought inside direct to the upper floor.

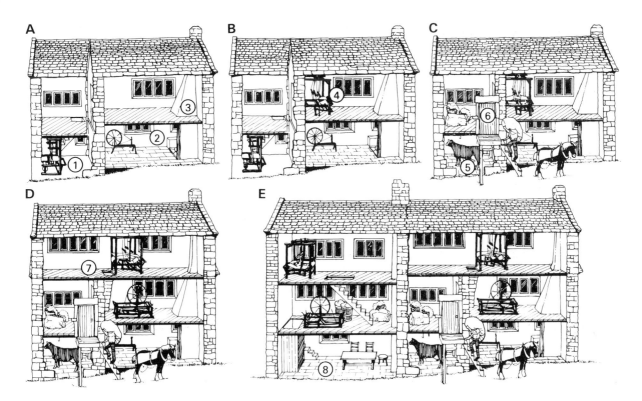

There may perhaps have been a ladder here, though in some houses there was a flight of steps leading up to the taking-in door instead. The door allowed employees who did not live on the premises to reach the workrooms without having to trespass on the privacy of their master's living-rooms, which were still entered directly from the main door. Once inside, the wool was carded and spun into yarn by the children and women of the family. Weaving proved to be ever more rewarding for the Buckleys, and production increased. So in 1795 they added another storey to both the original house and its extension to contain all the looms. This was given a band of thirteen windows to the front and smaller bands at the rear and in the gables. The room below was then used for carding and spinning and other processes.

There was to be yet a further stage in the development of the house as success followed success. In 1810 the Buckleys added what was in effect a complete second house to the first. Once more there were a pair of living-rooms in the ground storey, and two storeys of workrooms above, the lower for spinning, with a window of six lights and a taking-in door, the upper for weaving with a window of ten lights. The houses were probably occupied by two generations of Buckleys, father and son (just as today two generations of another family occupy them).

Weaving never entirely ousted cattle farming at Pinfold Farm, but it nearly did so. On the further side of the farmyard is a laithe, the typical Pennine type of barn designed to house both grain and cattle. Even here the upper storey, where the hay and straw for the cattle would normally be stored, was partly converted to a weaving loft. Today the weaving has all gone. The lofts are empty and have been for a hundred years, but Pinfold is still a farm, its fields covering the slopes leading up to the moor.

The five stages in the development of Pinfold Farm.
A: It started with an inner room (1) shown with a loom, and a firehouse (2) shown with a spinning wheel. The smoke from the fire escapes through a hood (3) and there are lofts in the upper storey. B: Next, the upper storey is raised to form a loom shop (4). C: Then the house is extended to provide a slaughter-house (5) and given a taking-in door (6). D: The next stage adds a third storey (7). E: In the final stage, a complete new house of three storeys (8) is added on the left-hand side.

In the hamlet of New Tame at Delph, there is a group of houses which together show all the changes in domestic architecture brought about by weaving that occurred around Saddleworth. The houses have a similar history to that of Pinfold Farm, though their development was on a significantly larger scale. New Tame is closer to the valley bottom where the fulling mills were built and so became far more prosperous. Here weaving took over from cattle farming entirely. Only remnants are left of the earliest house, which was probably a timber-framed farmhouse of the sixteenth century with a cruck frame. The first obvious evidence of building in stone at New Tame is a grand, six-light window with chamfered mullions and a hood-mould over it. It is the main surviving feature of another yeoman farmhouse, one from the seventeenth century that may well have been used for weaving. This house was rebuilt in 1742 by another Edmund Buckley, a yeoman who belonged to a richer branch of the family at Pinfold.

This Edmund Buckley turned New Tame into a small community of woollen clothiers during the latter half of the eighteenth century, and by the time he died in 1780, aged seventy-nine, he was no longer styled a yeoman but a 'clothier'. This change in status from yeoman to clothier can easily be seen by looking at the alterations he made to his home. He took down the upper floor of his house and rebuilt it as a higher loomshop with a new window of six lights in the front gable matching the one below. In this room Buckley could have accommodated four to six looms, together with a spinning jenny, a warping frame and other equipment necessary for making woollen cloth.

New Tame showing Edmund Buckley's house on the left, with its seventeenth-century window, and the houses that were progressively added as the community expanded in the later eighteenth century.

The long bands of windows at Dobcross, a potent reminder of the weaving industry that once filled the village with noise.

Edmund Buckley's Pinfold Farm at Saddleworth, showing on its exterior the stages of its enlargement.

Oakwood at Diggle, built by the Rhodes family as a farm and heightened to form a weaving loft. On the right is Dean Head, a purpose-built house with spinning and weaving rooms in the upper storeys. It was the last outpost of hand-weaving in Saddleworth and stayed in operation until 1912.

His success attracted fresh settlers to New Tame. There were three families living here in the 1780s and five, ten years later. They built additional loomhouses adjoining the Buckley one, the first reusing parts of an older house together with some new windows. The fourth house in the row is a fully purpose-built loomhouse of three storeys with a large loomshop on the top floor and a storage loft in the roof space. In order to bypass the living accommodation on the ground floor a taking-in door was built at first-floor level into the gable wall. It is now a large glazed window, but it and the long bands of windows still indicate the loomhouses that accommodated all the processes from carding and spinning to weaving.

These changes in both people's lives and their houses at New Tame as it developed from a farming community to a weaving community reflect the wider development of the cloth industry around Saddleworth. At first the weaving industry involved the whole family and used its own capital and labour, with perhaps an apprentice or two, and one or two servants or labourers, just as farmers had always done, and nearly all the processes of turning wool into cloth were accomplished within the house. An apprentice might start as a teenager and learn to spin, weave and dye the various kinds of wool and the cloths made from them; he would also learn to buy and sell. When he had finished his apprenticeship he might become a journeyman, travelling from job to job earning a wage until he was able to set up on his own as a master weaver.

When Edmund Buckley started building at New Tame in 1742, well over half the local output was still the coarse kersey. By 1790, however, most cloths were superfine broads, thanks to the introduction of Kay's fly-shuttle. In 1725 around 16000 cloths passed through the Yorkshire fulling mills. By the 1770s the number had reached 100000, and by 1795 it was a quarter of a million. In Saddleworth alone production doubled between 1740 and 1792 to exceed 36000 pieces. By then they fetched £7 each at Huddersfield, double what their price had been fifty years before. By the end of the eighteenth century West Yorkshire broadcloth was challenging the West of England product. This huge increase in the production of finished cloth meant that often the arrangements for selling it became completely inadequate. For example, in Huddersfield cloth used to be sold in the churchyard where the tombstones were used to display the pieces, but in 1766 a large cloth hall was built and it had to be enlarged in 1780 and again in 1864.

The development from small-scale production of kersey to large-scale production of broadcloth brought many changes. The clothiers who prospered and so built up their capital could afford to extend their houses and increase their loom capacity as Edmund Buckley did at New Tame. They then had to employ other weavers who had not the capital to do the same. These richer men became masters and employed a few journeymen. Soon some masters took on so many weavers and other employees that their houses in reality became small factories with paid workers outnumbering the labour of their own households or even entirely taking over from them.

Larger mills, as well as enlarged houses, demonstrate the consequences of the change from weaving kerseys to weaving broadcloth. Broadcloth needed more fulling to finish it, so fulling mills became

Shore Mill at Delph, built about 1782 when the slow process of industrialisation had just reached Saddleworth.

larger and some weavers and wool merchants with capital set up in business to run them and so provided a service to the locality's weavers. Other fulling mills were owned by groups of forty or fifty weavers who put up about £50 each to form joint stock companies for the purpose.

Mills for other purposes were built as well. Both kersey and broadcloth are made from short staple wool which had to be carded. This had long been a child's job, but around 1770 it too started to become mechanised and could be more efficiently undertaken outside the house in a carding or scribbling mill, to use the local name. Shore Mill at Delph was one of these. It was built in the early 1780s, perhaps in 1782, and was first known as Delph Willey Mill or Green Mill. (Willying, like scribbling, was a local name for carding.) Here, water powered a carding engine, one of Richard Arkwright's inventions of a few years beforehand, in which he had successfully mechanised the whole process of producing yarn from cotton. Now one of his inventions was applied to wool. It partly removed a process from the hands of the children who undertook it, and so increased the supply of wool for the spinners.

Shore Mill was the first indication in Saddleworth that the old economy was beginning to change. Despite its increasing prosperity, cottage industry was now under threat, though few recognised this at the time. Its demise still lay in the distant future. By the end of the eighteenth century weaving was no longer a simple family enterprise, entirely confined to the home, and farming, which weaving had first supplemented as an occupation, was now often forgotten. Villages of weavers' houses like Dobcross were built in the valley bottoms as near as possible to the fulling and carding mills, and few of them had any agricultural buildings. All the weavers needed was a stable for their packhorses because, as Defoe had seen earlier in the century, they required for the wool and cloth a 'prodigious number of people, horses, carts and wagons, to carry it from place to place'.

Meanwhile, down in the Lancashire plain, cotton was prompting the mechanisation of the weaving process. Where woollen broadcloth weaving was concerned, however, around Saddleworth, the handloom industry was still to continue for many decades and was the last to succumb to the Industrial Revolution. Kay's fly-shuttle had doubled the output of cotton weavers, and around 1770 Arkwright's spinning jenny redressed the balance by improving the rate of spinning the yarn to supply the looms. Soon jennies and looms were being powered by water mills, and then, in the 1780s, steam power was applied to cotton spinning and shortly afterwards to cotton weaving. Steam mills had arrived. By 1800 many of these were being built in Manchester and Salford because the coal for the steam engines was mined here and the water supply was good: all the other necessities could be brought in, the imported raw cotton on the one side and a human labour supply looking for the relatively high wages on the other. To accommodate these labourers densely packed streets of mean houses grew up. They were the most terrible slums in the country.

Where Manchester led, other weaving areas followed, but not without protests. Machines were wrecked. The masters who installed them were threatened and even murdered. The culprits were then hounded down and hanged. The Luddite Riots of 1811 and 1812, the tip of the iceberg, became commonly synonymous not so much with the misery of industrialisation as with the futility of opposing it. Those involved saw the machines as a threat to their livelihood as is obvious from this note, as terrified as terrifying, sent to a master clothier who had installed shearing machines:

> Wee Hear InFormed that you got shear in mee sheens and if you Dont Pull them Down in a Forght Nights Time Wee will pull them Down for you Wee will you Damd infernold dog.

It was much harder to mechanise the woollen industry than the cotton one, and broadcloth was harder to mechanise than the finer worsted. Worsted, which takes its name from the Norfolk village of Worstead, is a high-quality light cloth made from well-spun, long-staple wool. The industry grew up on the Pennines around Heptonstall, with markets in Halifax and Bradford. The houses of Heptonstall are significantly different from those of Saddleworth, although they too have long bands of windows. They are generally smaller and built as groups of similar houses in the form of terraces. Terraces had originated in towns, and were so fashionable by the later eighteenth century that they were commonly being built in villages. Nevertheless, the reason they can be found at Heptonstall is that they were cheaper to construct than

Terraces of small weavers' houses in Heptonstall, where worsted was made by the putting-out system.

individual houses, and enough people wanted the similar accommodation they provided to make it worthwhile building them. It happened here in particular because of the way in which the worsted industry was organised.

The whole worsted-making process was longer and needed five times as much labour as ordinary woollen broadcloth, and so cost much more. Only the richer men had the necessary capital to invest in it, so instead of the industry developing as a family affair, household by household, it was soon in the hands of capitalists. They put out the various processes of cloth-making to large numbers of hired workers. The raw wool was put out to the local children and women for combing and spinning, and then the yarn was put out again to the men for weaving. The clothiers worked to a fixed schedule of production for their convenience and profit, and paid their workers piece rates. This left the workers with little opportunity to direct their own lives. How much they worked and how much they were paid were out of their hands, and they had little spare time for farming. The uniformity of their lives and their lack of opportunity for individual enterprise is immediately reflected in their terraces of little uniform houses. So, well before the end of the eighteenth century the worsted spinners and weavers had reached a half-way stage between cottage industry and the factory system, years ahead of the broadcloth weavers. Although the worsted weavers still worked at home, they were not self-made men using their own capital but employees subject to the capital and economic requirements of the master clothiers.

The worsted industry was fully mechanised earlier than the woollen industry too. Even so, machines that could be powered by steam were very expensive, and it was only about 1800 that worsted production was largely undertaken in factories. Villages like Heptonstall stagnated economically then as the workers migrated to Hebden Bridge down in the valley where the new mills were concentrated beside the plentiful water supply of the River Calder, and where soon the new steam trains would be delivering their loads of coal to power them. The new mills moved closer and closer to the coalfields, and away from the central Pennines, the Yorkshire ones being concentrated further east around Halifax, Leeds, Bradford and Huddersfield.

Broadcloth took much longer to succumb to the machine and the factory system because at first the inventions assisted the handloom weavers. Between 1786 and 1806 the number of domestic cloth workers doubled and by the early nineteenth century there were about 65 000 people engaged in the Pennine cloth industry. Even as late as 1850 half of these workers were still engaged outside factories in domestic industry, mostly manufacturing broadcloth, and that was when the use of steam power in the West Riding had risen twofold between 1835 and 1850. Villages like the ones which make up Saddleworth were slowly transformed into towns. Yet a mixture of farming and weaving still kept some of its hamlets as small but thriving communities, at least in the good years.

Until the French Wars ended at Waterloo in 1815, broadcloth weaving was highly profitable. Yet not everyone succeeded. There were the failures, the poor, and by 1794 there was a workhouse in Saddleworth for them. A few years later a larger one was built and as this also proved inadequate it was replaced in 1815 by an even larger one whose ruins still stand on the heights of Broadstone Moss overlooking Diggle. The poor received soup and old herrings brought in for them from Hull, but they had to work for their food and shelter, for this was a House of Industry, and they were put to agricultural tasks and to carding and spinning.

When the wars ended in 1815 the demand for broadcloth collapsed. This was partly because the army no longer needed uniforms and blankets, but more generally, a series of economic depressions interspersed with short-lived booms made life difficult for farmers and industrialists alike. The old profitability of domestic weaving was gone, and the industry drifted in the doldrums at least until the 1830s. Looms were left idle, and the lofts emptied. Poverty stalked the packhorse trails to market. In the 1850s there were years when Saddleworth was a town of paupers. Spinners and weavers who had worked hard and lived frugally all their lives became destitute. Bands of them raided food shops in Manchester and Oldham. People called them 'the Saddleworth Mobbers'.

The workhouse filled up, and many weavers who still had their own homes but no work were given outdoor relief, the equivalent of today's supplementary benefit. There was little incentive to invest capital in machines because weaving broadcloth was so unprofitable. Nevertheless, the new water-powered and steam-powered mills picked off one stage after another in the industry, all the while encouraging the capitalist master at the expense of the self-financing families of spinners and weavers.

So for half a century mills like Shore Mill were only an adjunct to what remained essentially a domestic industry, kept going by a demand that no longer brought the great profits of the eighteenth century, but for a while was still strong enough to suspend the ultimate sentence on the home weaver.

The weavers who first felt the impact of the changing economy were those who lived high on the hillsides, away from the valleys where

Upper Slack Farm at Delph, one of many forlorn reminders of the farmer-clothier's lost prosperity.

the mills were being built. While the depression had made life difficult for them, mechanisation killed them. The Whiteheads of Upper Slack Farm, for instance, like the Buckleys, started off as farmers and became weavers, but they gave up weaving in the 1860s and moved away to make their living elsewhere. Their house has been empty for ninety years. Its ruins still bear their initials 'RW' and 'AW', a reminder of the good days of prosperity.

The transition from the home workshop to the factory was slow and hard. At the weaving hamlet of Diggle the hand looms were still at work in this century, and the weavers in one of the houses, Dean Head, did not give up until 1912. But more and more of the weavers and spinners of Saddleworth went to the mills. They worked at the company's machines, and earned a wage that kept them going. Sometimes they had to buy their food and clothing at the mill company's shop, and sometimes too they lived in the company's houses. These might be the notorious back-to-back terraces, though they were not necessarily as grim as they often tend to be painted. Small and cheap they were, but they could be solid, tolerably comfortable and decent. Above all, they were a far cry from the stinking, dank, packed tenements a few miles away in Manchester.

Close by the new Greenfield Mill in one of the Saddleworth valleys, the mill owners built a terrace of back-to-backs between 1820 and 1860 as they took on more labour. Eventually there were forty of them, so they came to be called 'Forty Row'. Even though the mill was just down the road, a communal weaving loft was built at one end of the row just as it might have been in the old days. From these houses, men, women and children were called by the mill bell to work long, hard hours. Their time, once regulated by the rising and setting of the sun,

The factory system comes to Saddleworth. Greenfield Mill with Forty Row behind it.

was now dominated by the unremitting demands of the machines and their employer. Yet the mill workers were neither completely in the mill's shadow nor without a view of the open countryside beyond.

How many of those workers saw that open country as symbolising the freedom that they had now lost? In 1837, C. Wing recalled in his *Evils of the Factory System* how people

> were taken from their cottages where they worked at their pleasure, with more or less intensity, and at a time when, in consequence of the demand for labour being greater than the supply, their wages were amply sufficient to maintain them, and placed in mills, where their labour was regulated by the machinery, and where sordid masters dictated what wages they chose, and what hours they chose.

It is a bleak view, and certainly not everyone suffered in this way. Yet the passing of domestic industry and the rise of the factory system crippled family life as it crippled the children. The miserable fact was that by this time only the factory could guarantee a living wage. It was left to the future to tackle problems in the factory and try to bring its conditions within what humanity could endure. Conditions in the mills were so dreadful that it was easy to be sentimental about the imagined pleasures of the vanished cottage industry and its weavers and spinners. In 1842 the *Halifax Guardian* remembered how:

> There was so much a home character in their little half farmstead, half clothing-shop; the master and his men and domestic apprentices were so much associated in friendly, almost family intercourse.

The living room of Spring Bank at Golcar, as it was furnished in the later part of the nineteenth century.

This communal life, at once domestic and industrious, must have had its pleasures though it was hardly Arcadia. These dark Pennine hills

Delph today; Shore Mill, in the foreground, is now a builder's store, and many of the later mills have been demolished or converted to other tasks.

only succour the hardy. Theirs was a harsh life, but it could be a good one, not crushing like life in the mills that pressed their way along the valley bottoms.

In the end the old life in the industrious home became more fragile than the houses it produced. The factories killed home industry, and our modern planning laws frown on residential and industrial zones being intertwined. Yet there has now been a kind of revenge on the factories, and it too has brought fresh hardship. There was once a railway running through Saddleworth bringing in coal to power the mills, and once every mill had its chimney and every chimney smoked as it made the steam to power the looms. They too were fragile. They too belong to the past.

CHAPTER FOUR
The Georgian Terrace

If appearances are anything to go by, the terrace house is England's most successful home. There are whole streets of terrace houses all over the country, many dating from the eighteenth and nineteenth centuries when speculators put them up in a frenzy of building never seen before. In the north London borough of Islington terraces run in all directions. They seem endless.

A few similar houses put together in a row make a terrace, and most Georgian terrace houses at least – that is those dating from around 1715 to 1835 – have much the same layout of rooms. But the terraces themselves come in all shapes and sizes. They can be long or short, curved to form a crescent or even a circus (a complete circle) or, more usually, grouped into a rectangle to form a square. They form England's most elegant streets, and their elegance is matched by their illustrious names. Royal Crescent, Grosvenor Square, Percy Circus, Windsor Terrace, Grafton Street, Bedford Row: these are the kind of names that suggest aristocratic origins and a dash of grandeur. That is the point of the terrace. The whole adds up to more than the sum of its parts. The whole terrace could be designed to look like a grand mansion, even a palace, not just a row of identical homes. It could be a place to live in style. There is plenty of style in Islington, but some of the terraces are a bit monotonous. Street upon street of houses, each the same as its neighbour, look a bit like a good idea exploited for all it is worth.

The terrace was more than just a good idea. It was a remarkable solution to the age-old, pressing urban problem of disordered building and overcrowding. Since the early Middle Ages towns had a special allure. They seemed to promise a very different life from the slow toil of agriculture in the countryside. There were quick profits to be made. The streets were proverbially paved with gold. The reality was of course different. Most people attracted to towns did not make fortunes and were often pressed together in great squalor. In towns, unlike the countryside, land is limited and therefore expensive, so you must build as much as possible on every site. This immediately raised problems of access and circulation, of heating and lighting, of construction and stability. Failure to solve these problems produced uncontrolled rookeries, houses jumbled together higgledy-piggledy on any vacant scrap of land. That was the cheap and easy way to put a roof over people's heads. It was also the cheap and easy way to spread disease and increase the risks of fire and collapse. Much of medieval London, the London burnt in the Great Fire of 1666, was like that, and it was out of this chaos that the terrace was born. But imposing order was not an easy business. In the first place, you had to own enough land to build on a large scale, so you had to be a landlord. As your terrace of houses would be more expensive than the ramshackle houses roundabout, there was also a financial risk. Would people want your houses enough to pay for them? So you had to be a speculator with capital to spend. The hope was that what you built would be superior, attract high rents and pay a handsome profit.

The first terraces were built in London as long ago as the fourteenth century, though they have long since been demolished. We have to go to towns like York, or Tewkesbury in Gloucestershire, or Battle in Sussex to see ordered terraces that are really old. All these early terraces were built by the Church, the largest landowner of all in the Middle Ages. The oldest survivors are in York. In about 1315 the vicar of Holy Trinity built a terrace of similar houses on the south side of his churchyard fronting Goodramgate. They served a need for accommodation at a time when the city's prosperity was expanding, and the rent was needed to support an increased number of priests. Some of the terrace still survives: seven two-roomed houses built to a uniform design.

Such uniformity was in direct contrast with the countryside. Houses there were generally built separately on individual plots. The occupiers were often closely involved in the building process and owned the houses even if they held a copyhold lease of the land rather than owned its freehold outright. In towns people seldom owned their houses, but rented them for as long as they wanted or could afford to stay. Often this was only a short time as mobility in towns was always far greater than in the countryside.

When the increasingly populous London burst at the seams in the seventeenth century, the wealthy landlords who owned many of the surrounding undeveloped estates saw the terrace house as a means of solving a number of problems: how to make the best profit from their land; how to provide a house that would serve the needs of a great variety of people; how to build in such a way as to enhance their new suburbs (and their names too, since they often gave them to their new streets and squares of terraces). They wanted to attract new, prosperous householders by giving them a good address. So the Earl of Bedford set to work outside the City at Covent Garden. Then came the Earl of Southampton and the Earl of St Albans. Other aristocratic landowners followed. Their names are littered around fashionable London to this day: Grosvenor, Harley, Cavendish, Chandos, Dartmouth. And so are the names of speculators who built terraces on land they had leased: Bond, Clarges, Frith, Neale and Panton. The most notorious of these men was the tricky Nicholas Barbon, an 'extremely able but far from amiable man', in Sir John Summerson's words, who devoured other people's money and land to invest £200000 in building all over the West End in the 1680s and 1690s. He saw the economic advantage of standardisation in that it eased the process of building, and also of standardised ornament as a means to attract the attention of the new bourgeoisie. This is how London began to creep out across virgin land, westwards away from the jostling City towards its daughter settlement of Westminster, and, rather more slowly, northwards towards Islington. All the while affluent people were pulled by the thought of an orderly life in a new salubrious suburb, and pushed by the desire to escape the chaos of run-down buildings which housed the working masses.

Islington was once a village of market gardens and dairy farms. Being so close to London there was a good market for its produce, and to the south were springs of clear water and the wells that attracted visitors from the City. It was also a pleasant place for anyone to visit who wanted to escape from the crowd. Some people came out here to live. The canons of St Bartholomew established a retreat to the north of the parish church in the Middle Ages and gave their name to modern Canonbury. Early in the eighteenth century there were already terraces of houses along the road to Highgate (Upper Street) and along the lower road to the hamlet of Newington (Essex Road). This was a form of ribbon development, already an age-old way for villages to grow. At Newington itself, a short terrace of four houses (Nos 52–55 Newington Green) had been built facing the Green as early as 1658, and they survive to this day as the oldest terrace of brick houses in London.

Things began to change in 1756 when London's first ring road was planned. This was the Marylebone New Road, which continued as Pentonville Road to Islington and then as the City Road into town. The route opened in 1761, and soon the stretches around Islington were being built up with shops and houses. Nevertheless, Islington managed to remain a village until near the end of the eighteenth century, but then London reached it, engulfed it as it engulfed so many other villages, and made it a suburb of terraces. By 1800, 10000 people lived here, and that number more than doubled in twenty years and then doubled again in the next twenty. Some people lived in terrace houses like the ones in Colebrook Row and Duncan Terrace; they are among the grandest terraces in Islington. But most people had to make do with something a good deal smaller. What they did not have to make do with was the disordered mass of houses that choked other parts of London. Landowners like the Rhodes family and speculators like the Colebrookes, who gave their name to Colebrooke Row, saw to that.

The progress of the Rhodes family almost symbolises the development of Islington itself. About 1800 Samuel Rhodes owned a dairy farm in what is now Duncan Street. There were some 500 cows and 400 acres of hayfields for them, a really sizeable farm. However, beneath those fields was a layer of brickearth, 5 to 7 feet deep, and that was more valuable. A tile kiln had already been established as early as 1727

Upper Street, Islington, early in the nineteenth century. The old houses on the right and the traffic in the street are still redolent of Islington the village, but on the left is one of the new terraces that was to change all that.

at the top end of Colebrook Row. Some ten years later there were brick and tile kilns in the fields to the east too, and a field on the west was called Clay Pit Field. The brick-making was then on a fairly small scale, but it was enough for Islington's needs. Even throughout the great building boom between 1800 and 1850 it remained adequate. By 1835 the Rhodes dairy farm had become one great brick field, the most productive in London, with bricks selling at £1 per thousand. An acre of clay could yield at least half a million bricks for every foot of its depth. That was enough to build ten fair-sized terrace houses and far more smaller ones. At a guess you could easily produce at least five times as many bricks as you needed for a house from the clay under the ground it would occupy. As for the Rhodes family, they were soon in the building business turning Islington, the village of dairy farms and pleasure grounds, into the suburb of bricks and mortar. 'Alas and well aday!' wrote John Nelson, the Islington historian in 1823,

> While the pen is recording the fleeting beauties of the spot, the demons of destruction, in the form of brick makers, road cutters, and sewer diggers, are despoiling the fair face of nature, and throwing the fields and their pathways into chaotic confusion.

Out of this confusion came rows and rows of ordered terrace houses.

The important thing about any house in a terrace is that it is a vertical slice of the complete terrace from the ground up to the roof. Every household has a fair share of all the advantages and disadvantages of building upwards so as to gain as much space on each narrow plot, and of having a front area, a back yard or garden and a number of floors from a basement or cellar up to the garrets. There are layers of use and a hierarchy of status immediately visible in the façade. For example, the basement at the bottom and garret at the top, the territory of the servants, are half hidden. The main living rooms on the ground and first floors have the tallest windows and the most decoration.

Having a number of rooms brought problems of access and circulation. These were aggravated when people began to want a modicum of privacy and were no longer prepared to reach a room only by going through another. This was even more important in London, where householders were less willing to live cheek by jowl with their servants. They could not have the servants running through all the rooms between the basement and the garret and disturbing them in the process. Rooms, therefore, had to be kept separate and given individual access from passages, stairs and landings.

The first stage in building a terrace house was to dig out the cellar. The soil from this excavation was often used to build up the roadway if it did not go to the brickmaker. Some town houses had even had cellars in the Middle Ages, and although these tended to be damp they did keep the rest of the house above more or less dry. In terrace houses the cellars were the main workrooms for the servants. There were usually at least two rooms, a kitchen and a scullery, and perhaps a number of smaller rooms for storing food, drink, crockery, cutlery and cooking implements. By the nineteenth century a coal cellar was often pushed out under the pavement in front of the house, and it could often easily be filled through a chute with a cast-iron cover fitting flush with the pavement, as you can still see today.

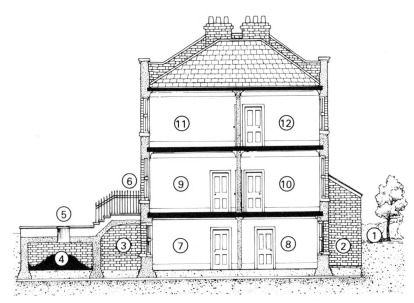

A section through a typical terrace house, showing: (1) ground level, (2) privy, (3) front area, (4) cellar, (5) coal hole in pavement, (6) front door, (7) kitchen, (8) scullery, (9) parlour, (10) dining room, (11 and 12) bedrooms.

Comparative plans of terrace houses showing changes in the position of chimneys and stairs. Top: houses of the seventeenth century based on Newington Green. Bottom: houses of the eighteenth and nineteenth centuries based on Brooksby Street.

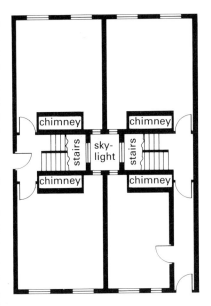

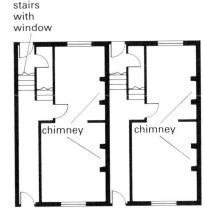

There would be a large kitchen range, a cast-iron fireplace with adjacent hobs and ovens, and usually a separate boiler for water and for washing. Sometimes houses had a rudimentary water supply, so there might be a pump, either indoors in one of the basement rooms or in the back yard, together with a stone sink. The yard was reached from the back room. It might contain a privy with an earth closet inside it, or even have a drain into a sewer. Beyond the yard, if there were space, would be a garden. Some terraces had a back lane for access, and grand houses might have a mews with stabling and coach-houses.

The ground floor of the typical terrace house was actually above ground level and often above the level of the made-up roadway as well. A few steps led up to the front door. From here a passage led down one side of the house to the stairs at the back. The passage was at first dark and gloomy, but the introduction of a window over the front door greatly improved matters. Often these windows were highly decorated with leaded patterns. Some were semicircular and had radiating patterns so giving us their generic name, fanlight. The passage gave access to a room at the front and another at the back. These might be a parlour and a dining-room, the main living rooms in a small house, but usage was not fixed and they could as easily be a bedroom and an office. Before about 1700 when the terrace house reached its fully developed form the staircase was placed between these two rooms. The worst thing about this position was that it was very dark. You could have a skylight in the roof, but that tended to leak, or you could have a light well and that wasted space. The terrace of 1658 at Newington Green has this latter form. Neither let much light through down to the ground floor. Placing the staircase against the rear wall where it could have a window of its own to light a half landing was an advantageous innovation.

The stairs led down to the basement and up to another pair of rooms on the first floor. In a small house these were usually bedrooms. In a larger one they might be formal reception rooms, drawing-rooms and parlours, and there were then bedrooms on the next floor above.

*Right and opposite page:
Islington fanlights, the first one
having a keystone decorated with
a head made from Coade stone.*

In either case there were closets between them, or tucked into spare spaces, or arranged in a projecting block on the back of the house. These closets were for clothing and the euphemistically named chamber-pots and closed stools that the servants had to spend so much time emptying. This was no longer often done directly into the roadway as it had been in earlier times with the notorious call of 'gardey loo' (mind the piss, discreetly put into French). Usually it was into an earth closet in the privy somewhere in the back yard or possibly directly into a drain. Sometimes the pots had to await the 'night soil man' who collected the soil – the excrement and household waste – and took it off to the local market gardeners for manure. By the nineteenth century various kinds of water-closet were available. The trouble was that they needed a reliable water supply and proper main drainage, and that only came in London after 1865.

Finally, in the roof space above the bedrooms came the garret. Here the servants had their cramped rooms, which they might have to share with a nursery for the babies. All the rooms in the house, except the closets and some in the garret, had fireplaces on the party wall away from the entrance passage and the stairs, and here was another source of hard work for the servants. The fireplaces were small, and fires regularly had to be cleared out and re-made. How many fires were kept burning at any one time is hard to judge. It was not just a question of how cold the weather was. A fire was no longer exactly a symbol of life, but it was at least a sign of hospitality. So a drawing-room or parlour fire might be kept going all year round for boiling kettles to make the newly fashionable pots of tea and to cook snacks.

Although all the rooms seem to have had clear-cut uses, there is no reason to believe that people adhered to those uses as closely as we do today. The order and regularity we see in the lay-out of the terrace house did not exactly govern people's lives.

That regularity and the classical proportions of the terrace-house façade go back to the 1630s when Inigo Jones, the architect who brought the Italian Renaissance style to England, designed London's first regular square of terrace houses for the fourth Earl of Bedford at Covent Garden. Jones took as his model the classical style of the great Italian architect Andrea Palladio. The base of his façade was an arcade of round arches like those Palladio had used in some of his town houses, and the upper storeys again followed Palladio by being embraced by tall classical pilasters that supported a cornice beneath the roof. Early builders copied Jones's design and included classical pilasters rising above a base formed by the ground floor. Soon, though, the pilasters were left out. They were expensive, and, although they were decorative and grand, their aesthetic purpose of emphasising the proportions of the front could be achieved more simply by grading the sizes of the windows and the gaps between them, up and down, and from side to side. This was fine on the upper floors, but did not always work on the ground floor with the arrangement of front doors and the windows adjacent to them. The practical requirement of placing the front door at the end of the entrance passage and the window centrally in the front room meant that they could not be made to tie in exactly with what was above. In the grandest terraces, pilasters might be retained, especially to mark out the centre houses or a group at each end, as a means of emphasising them. In Gibson Square in Islington the three end houses of the long sides are elaborately treated with larger windows and pediments as well as pilasters.

There is a great contrast between the ordered form of the terrace house and the seemingly chaotic way in which it was built. Today a builder will buy a piece of land, build houses on it and sell them to individual occupiers. That is relatively simple. From the time when the Earl of Bedford developed Covent Garden until well into the nineteenth century, building a terrace of houses was far more complicated. The original landlord might lease part of his estate to a speculator. The speculator might then find someone with ready capital, and mortgage the land to him so as to find the money with which to start operations. He would then hire a surveyor to lay out a street or a series of streets.

The frontages of the streets would then be divided into individual plots, and the speculator would lease them, either individually or in groups, to tradesmen from the building world, usually bricklayers or carpenters. One of these might provide the design of the terrace for all the other craftsmen to copy, if the speculator or his surveyor had not done so already. These builders would pay a nominal rent for the first year of the lease. Often this rent was in the form of a peppercorn, once a very valuable spice, but by the eighteenth century not individually worth very much. The payment of a peppercorn rent became a peculiar tradition required in a building lease and a means of instantly recognising one today.

The building tradesmen would guarantee to build a house on each plot within that first year so that it could be let out as soon as possible, and they would guarantee to build it in conformity with the overall design of the terrace. Nevertheless, they would probably not physically build it themselves, but employ lesser craftsmen who specialised in the various building trades and hired themselves out to do the actual job. They might not be paid in cash but instead barter their labour, and the

Building craftsmen of the eighteenth century.
Left: the brick maker.
Right: the bricklayer.

Duncan Terrace, one of Islington's grandest terraces, built to a uniform design, each house nevertheless being the work of a different tradesman from the building industry.

From market garden to brickfield. A view showing Kingsland Road and also the fate of much of Islington before house-building began.

*Classicism and the terrace house.
Below: Inigo Jones's prototype at
Covent Garden, built in the 1630s.
Right: Gibson Square, Islington,
still exploiting it nearly two
hundred years later.*

building materials they provided, for further building plots on which they could build themselves in the hopes of making a profit. Once a house was complete the builder would sell his lease together with the house, not necessarily to an actual occupier, but to someone who wanted to invest in houses. Only he would at last let off the house, often for a very short term, perhaps even for only a year, to an occupier. Meanwhile the original landlord still owned the land, gained an enhanced rent from it since it now had houses built on it, and knew it would revert into his full ownership at the end of the lease, a period which usually might be anything from about thirty to ninety-nine years.

All these numerous people from the landowner to the occupier could double their roles. For instance, the landowner could act as his own speculator, or the speculator as his own builder. With time many of these roles coalesced, and in the nineteenth century large firms of building contractors emerged to fill many of the central roles. Everyone involved in the building of terrace houses was hoping to make a profit, though in the rush to build there were many failures. With so many leases, subleases and mortgages, the courts were filled with disputes, and the lawyers did a roaring trade sorting out what everyone was supposed to be doing and who should pay how much to whom. The path from original landlord to the occupier of the completed house was long and tortuous and full of pitfalls, just the opposite of the clear-cut style of the terraces. The remarkable thing is that the system worked at all and that uniform terraces of houses could be built when so many people were involved.

In the seventeenth and eighteenth centuries this complicated procedure was undertaken in an informal fashion. The building tradesmen would receive fairly imprecise instructions, perhaps being told only to build in the form of houses already built, and given a few measurements. They would, as part of their skill, then do exactly what was expected of them. This was true of the bricklayer who built the carcass,

Building craftsmen of the eighteenth century.
Left: the carpenter.
Right: the plumber.

the carpenter and joiner who fitted the floors, roof, window frames and doorcases, the tiler and glazier who made the house weather-tight, the carvers who added the decorated porches, and so on.

By the start of the nineteenth century, however, this age-old craft tradition was breaking down. The architectural profession was beginning to dominate design and to give increasingly precise instructions, together with drawings, for what it wanted. The individual skills of the master craftsmen declined as their powers of invention were circumscribed, and they were forced into producing either what had been designed by the architects or what appeared in numerous pattern books. Some managed to develop their entrepreneurial skills, and widened the scope of the building work they contracted to do. But the economic position of most craftsmen declined with their skills. No longer could they work for themselves, but instead had to seek work wherever they could find it from the new building contractors who came to dominate the market. The old craftsmen became mere journeymen, taking what work they could and often only by accepting the lowest of wages. There was no redress. If you held a meeting together with even a few of your fellow craftsmen you could be accused of forming a combination, and that was against the law and brought the possibility of three months in prison. It was not just the fear of strikes and the ruination of an uncomfortably fluctuating economy that lay behind this punitive law, but the notion that revolution was only just around the corner. The dreadful lesson of the events in France was fresh in everyone's minds.

The craftsmen were not only squeezed out by the speculators and building contractors who were looking for quick profits. Both taste and the implementation of building regulations made houses conform to increasingly standard patterns, and that did not help the craftsmen either. On top of this, the Napoleonic Wars that started in the 1790s upset the economy by causing interest rates to rise. This made it hard to borrow money for building. Then the trade cycle of deep recessions followed by short-lived booms that continued until 1850 made building harder still. Because houses absorbed much capital, a wise man tried to judge the market and build while interest rates, and the prices of building materials and wages were low in the expectation of an upturn in the market. He could then sell his completed houses at the peak of demand when all these costs had become inflated, as had the prices that he could charge. If you judged the market wrongly you would find yourself building not the desirable, cheap terrace houses that people would flock to fill, but instead a debtors' prison to set around your shoulders. This ebb and flow of supply and demand caused the cost of houses to be pared down to a minimum. Jerry-building, if you could get away with it, had many attractions. Even so, there were inevitably many bankruptcies among capitalists and extreme personal hardship among the men who did the building. A man who called himself a craftsman in the middle of the eighteenth century might be a mere labourer if he had lived a century later.

To set against the jerry-builder were the building regulations. They came into being for a different reason, in fact from a desire to control the size of the City of London. A Royal Proclamation of 1580 had forbidden all building within 3 miles of the City and so created the first green belt. It was to circumvent this that the Earl of Bedford used the architect Inigo Jones in the 1630s for the design of Covent Garden. His terraces would be built within this green belt, but they would also be a monument to enrich the City. So the Crown made an exception to the Proclamation and granted a special licence allowing him to build 'howses and buildings fitt for the habitacons of Gentlemen and men of ability'. The licence laid down just how the houses were to be built, specifying materials, dimensions and other details.

General regulations of the same kind immediately followed the Great Fire in the Act for the Rebuilding of the City of London of 1667. It was the real forerunner of modern building regulations. With the need to avoid the spread of fire foremost in the legislator's minds, the Act insisted that all new building must be of brick or stone, and that its height must be limited by the widths of the streets that it fronted. 'For better regulation, uniformity and gracefulness' houses were to be graded into four classes, and standards of construction were specified for each. Three of these classes referred specifically to terrace houses and actively promoted their uniform and graceful qualities. The type of street in which the houses were to be built was also specified. Classes of houses were thus to be segregated in their own streets.

There were to be no more building Acts after 1667 until the early eighteenth century. The 1707 Act 'for the better preventing mischiefs that may happen by fire' required party walls to have parapets above the roof line and made wooden eaves illegal. Instead, there had to be brick parapets. In 1709 another Act required further precautions against fire, and stipulated that window frames be set back from the face of the house by 4 inches, the thickness of a brick. As fashions changed, houses were beginning to have parapets instead of wooden eaves cornices anyway, and recessed window frames instead of flush frames as these helped to emphasise the lines of a façade and give it a feeling of body. So it is hard to know whether it was aesthetic or legal considerations that determined London's terrace-house façades.

The Building Act of 1774 was especially concerned with sound construction and outlawing the jerry-builder. It determined the thickness of party walls, always a bone of contention. An unscrupulous builder working for a crafty speculator could easily use the party wall of a neighbouring house to support his floor joists when it was only firm enough to support its own. The dimensions of party walls and external walls were now specified in great detail, and construction was to be checked and certified by District Surveyors. To do this, buildings were categorised into seven rates. Four of them applied to terrace houses, and, because the rates were fairly precisely stated, houses came to be known by the rate to which they conformed. The rates of houses were defined by floor area, value, number of storeys and height above ground level. These seemingly specific definitions were open to much interpretation and could be contradictory. A fourth-rate house, for instance, could comply with the regulations in its value and floor area yet be higher and have more storeys than the amount specified. Many fourth-rate houses were built in poor parts of Islington at the start of the nineteenth century. They provided limited accommodation and were an unrewarding investment, so few survive today. Larger houses were a better speculation. By the 1850s, when their pristine novelty

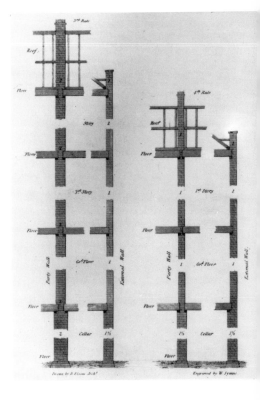

A guide to wall construction for houses of the third and fourth rates, from Peter Nicholson's The New Practical Builder and Workman's Companion *of 1823.*

The four rates of houses as defined by the Building Act of 1774.
From left to right: A first-rate house in Bedford Square, a second-rate house in Canonbury Square, a third-rate house in Charlton Place, and a fourth-rate house in Brooksby Street.

had worn off, they were often subdivided for multi-occupation. Even so they had a better chance of surviving.

Mindful of the ever-present menace of fire, the legislators of the 1774 Act attended to the external appearance of houses too by banishing projecting wooden porches and by requiring the sash boxes of windows to be rebated into the inner faces of the walls, thereby becoming all but invisible from outside. A major consequence of the Act was that in future the decoration of a terrace-house façade was limited to what could be done in stucco and decorative ironwork. The exuberance of the earlier Georgian period was banished, but taste had moved in the direction of a sober neo-classicism anyway. In this case the law was as much following taste as leading it. A cheap, undecorated house was very plain indeed, and the Victorians of the next century were to complain strongly about the mass of monotonous grey terraces that ringed London. Nevertheless, it was still possible for stuccoed porches and cast-iron railings and balconies to give a terrace a strong feeling of grandeur.

Since the Elizabethan age taste had been influenced by architectural illustrations. These reached their heyday in the later eighteenth and nineteenth centuries. Pattern books of architectural features were eagerly sought by building craftsmen to provide them with inspiration if not actual designs for the features with which they would ornament their houses. The books applied to the whole range of crafts employed in house-building, and the result of this copying was ever greater uniformity of design and the mass production of ornament. As early as 1703 a bricklayer who was responsible for the carcass of a terrace house could turn to Joseph Moxon's *Mechanick Exercises* for instruction on where to underpin his walls with piers and how to set up chimney-stacks and their flues. The same author provided a popular interpretation of the whole vocabulary of classical architecture in his *Vignola or the Compleat Architect* of 1702. Terrace-house builders only started to involve themselves with the niceties of classical architecture after the

middle of the eighteenth century. Here they were helped by Isaac Ware's influential *A Complete Body of Architecture* published in 1756, while William Halfpenny's *The Modern Builder's Assistant* of 1742 and 1757 provided exemplars of a variety of houses.

There were also changes in the brickwork of terrace houses over a period of time. At the start of the eighteenth century, a warm plum-red brick was standard for houses and had been since Jones's time. Lighter red bricks were used for pilasters and to surround window and door openings and give them emphasis. High-quality bricks were used for arches over the openings and sometimes as aprons beneath their sills. They were moulded, carved or rubbed to shape and occasionally given projections in the form of keystones in the centre of the arches. After the 1707 Act a carved brick cornice might take the place of a wooden one beneath the parapet. In the middle of the eighteenth century, however, much of this carving went out of fashion, and yellow-grey bricks took the place of the exuberant reds. People thought they looked more like stone, which they held in higher regard than brick.

The bricklayer's carcass had to be fitted out by a house-carpenter with floors and roof. This traditional work also became the subject of pattern-book writers like Peter Nicholson, whose *The New Practical Builder and Workman's Companion* was published in 1823. This helped the increasing number of less skilled carpenters to learn their trade as the old masters were forced out of business and facilitated the mass production of timbers cut to standard lengths.

The pattern books supplemented the Building Acts' efforts to maintain sound construction. Even so, many builders found ways to save money by going round the law and concealing the fact from the District Surveyors. Sometimes they were found out when their buildings collapsed. What really advertised a terrace, though, was not so much sound construction as good decoration. In even modest houses a joiner or carver might supply highly decorative bracketed porches in the style of Grinling Gibbons, the joy of any house early in the eighteenth century. Inside, he would fit the staircase with twisted 'barleysugar' balusters and a moulded rail. He would panel the walls as wallpaper was still too expensive, and fit wooden moulded cornices. All this was fairly standard, but there were different degrees of enrichment for the mouldings. Then came the windows. Since the Great Fire, sliding sashes had become increasingly popular and had ousted the old-fashioned casements, first at the front where they would be seen, then at the back. In the first sashes only the upper section was movable and it needed to be propped open, but by 1700 a system of cords and weights set in boxes beside the grooves in which the sashes slid counterbalanced both windows, open or shut. Internal wooden shutters covered the principal windows at night. They usually folded into boxes at the sides of the window frames, though some were hung vertically like sashes and rose out of a box at the base of the window. Blinds and curtains started to replace shutters only in the nineteenth century.

Towards the middle of the eighteenth century, just as red bricks were giving way to yellow, the exuberance of the carved woodwork gave way to a tamer and more correct classicism. It incidentally produced a doorcase with pilasters or columns and an entablature or perhaps a pediment that no doubt pleased academic sensibilities, but was not always so good at protecting you from the rain. There were plenty of illustrated books for instruction here, going right back to those by Italian Renaissance architects like Serlio and Palladio which had by now been translated into English. But James Gibbs's *Book of Architec-*

The frontispiece of one of Batty Langley's numerous pattern books.

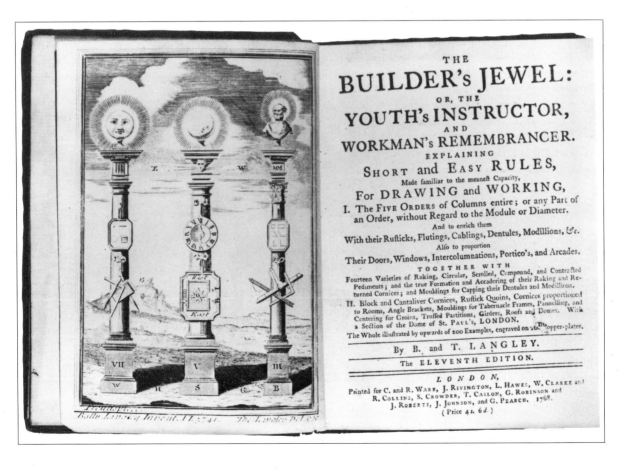

ture of 1728 was usually good enough, and Batty Langley's numerous designs, many of them plagiarised from other designers and published in the numerous editions of books like *The Builder's Director*, had the common touch.

All this external timberwork was, of course, forbidden by the Act of 1774, but by then it was no longer fashionable. Stucco outside, plaster inside and the first readily available mass-produced wallpapers gave houses a new appearance. From about 1760 architectural taste had been decisively changed by two men, Sir William Chambers and Robert Adam. Both were inspired directly by Ancient Rome rather than by a second-hand interpretation as the earlier Palladians had been. Chambers was at once professional and professorial. His travels had stretched as far as China and led to the construction of the audacious pagoda at Kew, but as a learned classicist he was without equal. He published the essence of his knowledge in his *Treatise of Civil Architecture* in 1759.

Robert Adam was very different. He was disinclined to apply the academically correct forms of classical temple architecture to houses – after all, the Romans themselves had not done so – but instead preferred to decorate them with motifs taken from ancient houses, and in a far gayer and more light-hearted manner. When Robert and his brother James Adam published their designs in a series of volumes called *Works in Architecture* starting in 1773, they could truly write, 'We have adopted a beautiful variety of light mouldings, gracefully formed, delicately enriched and arranged with propriety and skill.' Their combination of flowing swags and ribbons, of garlands of honeysuckle blossom, and of fretworks of abstract classical forms became instantly fashionable, not just for architectural features – façades, doorways, gables, cornices and so on – but for chimney-pieces and ceilings, for furniture and even for porcelain. From 1768 Robert Adam's London buildings, a handful of terrace houses in Portland Place and Fitzroy Square and, most importantly, the Adelphi, became exemplars of taste. They showed how the new forms of decoration could be applied to stucco and cast iron, while *Works in Architecture* and the Adams' publication of drawings made in Italy and Dalmatia provided details of their sources. This fashion was rapidly taken up by builders and formed the basis of their decorative work for at least half a century.

Great advances were made in developing cements or stuccoes to provide a waterproof coating to a building, adhere properly to the brickwork, and give the illusion of being stone, especially if they were stippled with paint. They also provided a basis for moulded decoration (which was cheaper than carved wood) and was fireproof. Many inventors rushed their individual mixtures to the Patent Office and went into partnership with builders, as John Liardet did with the Adam brothers. His stucco was not a great success, though it is fair to say that their relationship became even more quickly unstuck than the cement. The most lasting decorative material was Coade stone. Its appearance on the market coincided with the 1774 Act, and it had a runaway success. It was not its excellent lasting qualities that sold it, but its timely appearance and the artistry of the designs you could obtain in it. It was a success made all the more singular because it was achieved by a woman, an unheard of occurrence in the building industry.

A doorway from Eleanor Coade's catalogue of 1778, showing rusticated quoins, classical mouldings and a keystone with a head as used in Bedford Square (see page 92).

The Coade Artificial Stone Manufactory opened in Lambeth in 1769 to produce decorative mouldings made from a mixture of clay and sand that was then fired in a kiln to produce a hard ceramic. The owner and manager of the works was Eleanor Coade, assisted by her cousin and partner, John Sealy. They employed many famous sculptors for their designs. Eleanor was herself a modeller in clay, and she provided some of the distinctive designs that formed the basis of the castings that made the firm famous and her name a household word. The firm supplied everything from small rusticated blocks for door surrounds to large, ornate, decorative relief panels. Their most endearing work is comparatively modest: a series of keystones decorated with heads of gods and goddesses, satyrs and animals. These and much of their work were obtainable through their sales catalogue. Their goods were not expensive. While you could spend the princely sum of 100 guineas on a river god from the 1784 catalogue, Ionic capitals were only 13s each, and a frieze of griffins came at 10s a foot. Their work was justly popular and was exported eastwards to Poland and Russia, and westwards to the United States. In London many a house had its doorway or windowhead picked out with decorative features taken from the Coade catalogue.

Unlike Coade stone, the interior equivalent, plaster, remained a job for the independent plasterer, though once again individual decorative items of plaster had been mass-produced as early as the sixteenth century and could be fixed on site. Ornate rosettes, modillions, blocks, paterae and other details could be cast and then fixed into a classical cornice, which was run by the plasterers directly onto the join between wall and ceiling. From the middle of the eighteenth century the models were taken from the publications of Chambers and the Adam brothers. There were alternatives to the classical style in what Chambers brought back from his visit to China and in what Batty Langley thought he had observed from the Middle Ages. Such Chinese or Gothic decorations gave a room a special flavour, and you could even put them all together like an ice-cream sundae into a wonderful confection of mysterious romance.

Walls too began to be plastered as panelling went out of fashion in the eighteenth century. A skirting board, dado and dado rail remained for a while serving the classical function of providing a base to balance the cornice above, and the practical one of resisting bumps and scrapes. The rest of the wall might be limewashed, and blue copper sulphate or green iron sulphate could be mixed into the wash to deter mildew. Eventually these pastel colours became fashionable for themselves, and their practical origins were forgotten. Some walls were painted with scenes, *trompe-l'oeil* architectural effects or merely stencilled. Wallpaper, a cheap form of the rich, earlier hangings of leather, tapestry or silk, was already obtainable from Edward Batling of Southwark in the 1690s. But it was taxed at the high rate of 1d and later $1\frac{1}{2}d$ per square yard, and it was not until the later eighteenth century that it came into popular use. Hand-blocked abstract patterns, floral designs and exotic or rustic scenes were all popular.

In the seventeenth and early eighteenth centuries houses were guarded from the road by wooden posts. Only a grand house would have expensive wrought-iron railings, sometimes with gates and elaborate patterns of shaped iron *repoussé* work, which was the individual work of smiths. It was the founder, with his ability to mass-produce in cast iron, who brought the price of ironwork within the reach of all in the later eighteenth century. Again it was classical taste and the impetus of the 1774 Act that made cast iron an indispensable element of all but the meanest terrace. Railings and gates, lampholders, and above all window balconies provided a wonderful opportunity for a fretted array of cast iron. The best source was Lewis Cottingham's *The Smith and Founders' Directory* of 1824, though it was only reflecting the neoclassical taste in cast iron established by the Adam brothers some fifty years before.

By 1824 the old vernacular traditions of building were dead in the towns and quickly dying in the countryside. Even there terrace houses had become popular. They were cheap to build and fashionable. Everywhere locally made materials and designs were being replaced by cheaper

Running a cornice. The international award-winning plasterer John Joy at work. Fresh plaster is being added on the left while the template is moulding it into shape from the right.

Cast-iron balcony rails from Lewis Cottingham's The Smith and Founder's Directory *of 1824*

Patterns for Window Guards and Balcony Railing executed in London.

ones brought in by canal. Soon the railway could take a cheap load of bricks anywhere and, for that matter, an architect too, a member of a rising profession who knew the latest styles. Local builders were usually ready to copy him even if they did not directly employ him.

When at last a house was complete, a tenant had to be found to occupy it. Advertisements appeared in newspapers and in local public places, for there was not yet a developed system of house agents. Early in the nineteenth century annual rents for houses of the second and third rates might be anywhere between about £80 and £200, depending on the locality and the level of demand. A low rent was set at about a tenth of the value of a house, though ground rent and other charges increased the amount. With so many types of terrace house, occupiers came from many stations in life. They might be worth £50 or £50000. They might be artisans or ambassadors. In Islington there was a great mixture of people and still is. Everyone was glad to come to Islington. It was near the City, near the countryside, stylish and convenient.

Families often had three, four or five children. The poorer kept a single servant. The richer more usually had three – namely, a cook, a general maid, and either a manservant or a nurserymaid. After agricultural work, domestic service was the largest occupation in the middle of the nineteenth century. The servants paid the highest price for the advantages of the terrace house. In a four-storeyed house there might be fifty steps between their garrets and their workrooms in the basement. Noting this, the American traveller Louis Simond made a telling comparison between the Parisian apartment and the London terrace house: 'An apartment all on one floor, even of a few rooms only, looks much better, and is more convenient,' he wrote in his journal for 1810–1811. But in London:

> These narrow houses, three or four stories high – one for eating, one for sleeping, a third for company, a fourth underground for the kitchen, a fifth perhaps at the top for the servants – and the agility, the ease, the quickness with which the individuals of the family run up and down, and perch on the different stories, give the idea of a cage with its sticks and birds.

Nevertheless, Simond recognised the advantages of being independent of your neighbour's noise, dirt, diseases and dangerous fires – in short, of having a complete home. He found the common entrance and stairs of French apartments abominably filthy, whereas the neat, compact and independent entrances of English terraces were clean and orderly,

The hall and acrobatic staircase of a house in Compton Terrace.

the houses 'snug and comfortable'. Was Simond really so unfamiliar with the Georgian terrace house? Like many other forms of English architecture, the terrace was taken up in the United States, and many towns and cities on the eastern seaboard have streets of what Americans call 'row houses' as grand as those of Islington.

Today few of these houses have servants. Instead they have the amenities of running water and main drainage, of gas and electricity, and so of bathrooms with hot and cold water, and lavatories with water-closets, of central heating throughout the house. The terrace house is now much easier to run. Hods of coal and ashes, jugs of water and pots of excrement are not continually going up and down stairs. The stairs may still be the penalty for a snug and comfortable home, but in larger terrace houses at least they are an elegant part of the design that matches the well-proportioned rooms and façades. These values matter to some people, and so terrace houses remain popular. Since the great change from rented occupation to home ownership, especially after the Second World War, terrace houses have found a seemingly inexhaustible market, just as they had when first built. An address in an Islington terrace in the 1980s is a source of pride.

A hundred years ago it was different. The Victorians found all those plain-fronted houses extremely enervating. Their own terraces were often enlivened with great quantities of stucco, contrasting grey, yellow, red and black bricks, projecting porches and bay windows. Vigour was the Victorians' watchword, not elegance. Nevertheless, the Victorians recognised that the terrace was good value for money. There was something to be said for the way in which it could be mass-produced; and mass-produce it they did, with richly decorated façades for the affluent professional classes who needed a good address, and as plain as plain for the masses who tended their factories.

CHAPTER FIVE
Two-up, Two-down

The terraces of our northern industrial towns stand rank upon rank like a mute army drawn up before the factories that once commanded them. They were a symbol of the urban proletariat that was called into being to serve the cause of the Industrial Revolution: now they are becoming its memorial. Massive armies are not easily disbanded, yet in the last generation this army has started to fade away as the industries that created it die one by one.

From the start there was the romantic aura of a heroic struggle about these places. 'To travellers descending from the moorland, the smoke and roar of Lancashire seemed like the smoke and roar of a battlefield, and the discipline of the factories like the discipline of a great army', recorded the historian G M Young in his *Victorian England: Portrait of an Age* (1936). That industrial battlefield is now quieter, its smoke more intermittent, but its streets of houses are a potent source of both social research and popular fiction. Mythical towns like Weatherfield bring them into our living-rooms, but the reality is still plain to see in Preston, Salford, Bolton, Rochdale and Nelson, and in the greatest of them, Manchester.

An aerial view of Preston in 1946, filled with mills and terraces right to the horizon.

In all of these places, and all over Lancashire, there are terraces of crowded little houses with two rooms upstairs and two down, and many more with extensions jutting out into their back yards giving the houses a room or two extra. Despite being small and crowded, these terraces were a great improvement on the disease-ridden courts of foetid tenements that first housed Lancashire's workers and most industrial workers elsewhere. But this was only because pressure for reform and social legislation had managed to force those who built the terraces to include basic sanitary arrangements.

These Lancashire towns, the spearhead of the Industrial Revolution, came into existence to serve cotton. In 1780 they were little more than villages, for at that time practically all cotton still went to hand spinners and weavers working in their homes. Seventy years later their domestic industry had become a mere shadow. Instead 300000 operatives served the new mills. In that period the population had surged forward from seven and a half to eighteen million, the production of cotton had gone ahead ten times more rapidly to satisfy the home market, and at the same time accounted for a third of the value of exports as well. The towns that achieved this were on the map, and Wordsworth saw them,

> . . . continuous and compact.
> Hiding a face of earth for leagues – and there,
> Where not a habitation stood before,
> Abodes of men irregularly massed
> Like trees in forests, – spread through spacious tracts,
> O'er which the smoke of unremitting fires
> Hangs permanent.

(The Excursion, 1814)

When Wordsworth died in 1850 the inhabitants of these towns were slowly coming to appreciate the shocking reality of those irregularly massed abodes of men created in their midst. The first of the serried ranks of ordered terraces built round the nucleus of the mills and disordered dwellings were already there. These were in direct contrast to the labyrinth of narrow alleys, and close, airless courts of jam-packed rooms and cellars that filled once spacious yards and gardens. Even so, initially they were less of a solution to the workers' housing needs than they appeared to be.

Preston, rather than Weatherfield, shows what happened. In 1795, according to J Aikin's *A Description of the Country . . . round Manchester*, this was still 'a handsome well-built town, with broad regular streets and many good houses . . . rendered gay by assemblies and other places of amusement, suited to the genteel style of the inhabitants' – in short, a 'rendezvous of fashion and society'. In 1777 cotton spinning had been introduced to the town and by 1801 its population of 6000 had doubled and continued to rise quickly as spinners and weavers were attracted there by the prospect of work and good wages. By 1851, 68000 people inhabited the town.

Preston had started with three wide streets: Church Street ran east from the centre, Fishergate ran west, and Friargate curved north-westwards. They were once lined with inns and tradesmen's houses, and behind them were long narrow courts and gardens typical of urban landholdings. But by 1800 the houses were being subdivided and their courts were starting to be filled in with buildings haphazardly run up to meet the demand of the increasing population. What new houses were built tended to be small and cramped. This was largely a consequence of the French wars of 1793–1815 which had resulted in a steady increase in the price of building materials and also a rise in interest rates. As up to two-thirds of the cost of a house was in interest charges, the size and basic amenities of those built in towns like Preston were drastically curtailed in the hope of making economies and keeping costs down. Besides, house building had to compete with industry itself for capital investment, and industry was more profitable here. The once open courts were soon choked with poor dwellings, the dwellings with people. Access to the courts and what open spaces were left within them was restricted to the narrowest of alleys in a desire to obtain the maximum accommodation. Sanitary conditions within the courts were foul. A water supply often did not exist, and where it did was seldom more than a well or single pump. Open drains were

The entrance to New Cock Yard, Preston. Immediately behind the elegance of the Georgian houses were once gardens, but by the 1820s there was nothing but the squalor of overcrowded dwellings.

Early nineteenth-century houses packed down one side of a Preston alley. The houses that lined the other side and made a canyon of the alley have been demolished, so it is hard to visualise how dark and airless they all were.

everywhere. Refuse piled up high: it was hard to remove and no one's responsibility to do so. The courts were dark and damp, and plagued with disease.

These conditions were eventually recorded, as reports of Preston in 1849 show. They compare grimly with pleasant descriptions of the town fifty years earlier. As the local inspector of the recently established Board of Health explained:

> Turk's Head-yard, on the south side of Church-street, is a long irregular alley, rather narrow, paved and without efficient drains. Here are several filthy corners, and a very large cesspit, said to be the largest in the town, receiving the contents of six privies. Close by is a large slaughter-house in a dirty condition and giving out a most offensive smell.

Next on the south side of Church Street came Bolton's Court. It had

> a range of piggeries and open dung-heaps, with a large trough for the storing and mixing of manure. Near is the National School with 700 or 800 children, and on the opposite side are the gas-works, once in the suburb, but beyond which the town has rapidly spread. In Bolton's-court are also eight public slaughter-houses.

At the bottom of these two courts lay a cotton mill, and between them were packed numerous dwellings. They were the first slums, a word that seems to have been coined here in the North and was first applied to these overcrowded courts early in the nineteenth century. (Its origin is obscure, but may be the same as 'slump', northern dialect for a mire.)

Near the slaughter-houses in Bolton's Court was George's Row, twelve little houses, eight of them built back-to-back and perhaps with further dwellings in their cellars. These cellars had originated as weaving rooms. Unlike wool, cotton needs damp conditions for weaving, because it becomes too brittle when dry, and cellars were ideal for this despite their poor lighting. As handloom cotton weaving fell before the onrush of the mills, the cellars were taken as dwellings by the new factory operatives, here and everywhere in Lancashire. As a Manchester surgeon, John Robertson, told the Committee on the Health of Towns in 1840:

> The number of cellar residences, you have probably learned from the papers published by the Manchester Statistical Society, is very great in all quarters. . . . That it is an evil must be obvious on the slightest consideration, for how can a hole underground of from 12 to 15 feet square admit of ventilation so as to fit it for a human habitation?

Clearly some sort of action was needed.

The appointment of the Committee was the first official step taken in Victorian England to tackle the terrible legacy of housing bequeathed by the Industrial Revolution to the nation's factory workers. Their standard of living had been slowly slipping since the beginning of the century, not as a gradual decline, for there had been good years like 1825 and 1835, but as a series of plunging steps like those of 1817 and 1842 when food was dear, work scarce and pay low. Robertson emphasised this in his evidence:

So long as [Manchester] and other great manufacturing towns were multiplying and extending their branches of manufacture and were prosperous, every fresh addition of operatives found employment, good wages, and plenty of food. . . . Now, however, the case is different. . . . It is in a much depressed state of the manufacturing districts as at present exists that unpaved and badly sewered streets, narrow alleys, close, unventilated courts and cellars, exhibit their malign influence in augmenting the sufferings.

There seemed, Robertson asserted, to be no hope of a remedy:

New cottages, with or without cellars, huddled together row behind row, may be seen springing up in many parts. . . . With such proceedings as these the authorities cannot interfere. A cottage row may be badly drained, the street may be full of pits, brimful of stagnant water, a receptacle of dead cats and dogs, yet no one may find fault.

Even so, the rows of these cottages or small houses were not always bad in themselves and they were increasingly being run up in the 1840s to meet the demands of the mills as workers flocked to Preston. The best of them were solidly built and had some of the typical elegance of terrace houses elsewhere, but many were so tightly crowded together on every narrow strip of land that living there was only marginally better than in the slum courts.

Each house generally had two rooms on both of its two floors (hence the term 'two-up, two-down'), sometimes a cellar, and nearly always its own privy in a back yard. For the most part, the accommodation was arranged as a pair of bedrooms over a living room at the front and a wash-house at the back.

The internal arrangements were similar to those of terraces everywhere, even though on a very small scale. The smallest houses had their entrances opening straight into the front room with a small partition to reduce the draught from the front doors. This was a

One of Preston's traditional corner shops, typical of all industrial towns where two-up, two-down houses abound.

*Cutaway perspective of a two-up,
two-down terrace house, showing
the living room with cooking
range at the front, wash-house
with 'set-pot' at the back, and two
bedrooms above.*

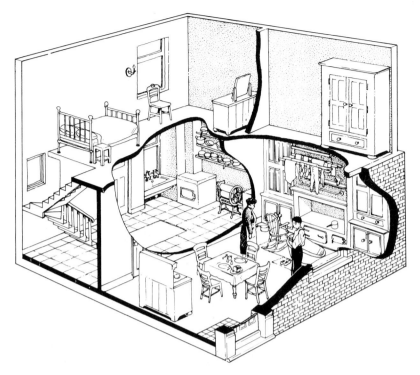

distant descendent of the seventeenth-century heck, though it was
now called by the southern word, spere. There was seldom a passage-
way to the back that would give the individual rooms some privacy.
The front room was the main living room. It had a fireplace for cooking
and a doorway leading into the back room, the wash-house. Here there
was a water boiler or 'set-pot' built into a corner. This was an iron
water bowl with a wooden lid, set in a brick structure with a hearth
beneath it and a flue above. It heated water for all the washing, both of
the clothing and the occupants. Everyone bathed in a tin tub in the
front room, so you could not expect much privacy. Another tub in the
shape of a dustbin was used to wash clothes in, which were then dried
on a line either in the yard or the passageways that led to them. If you
could afford to pay for the convenience, there were the Public Baths
and Wash-houses in Saul Street, built by Preston Council in 1850.
Only those who lived close by used them.

The wash-house had a door to the back yard and the stairs to the
bedrooms. In a large family male children might have to sleep in the
living room for the sake of propriety, as it was not respectable for
adolescent brothers and sisters to sleep together. In a small family, one
of the bedrooms might be used for a lodger to help with the rent
(though this was unusual in Preston). The front bedroom had a
fireplace, but not the back one. The upstairs fire was usually only lit
when one of the women was in confinement. The fireplace in the
living-room that served for cooking was usually 4 feet wide and might
have taken an open basket grate in the centre with flat hobs each side
and a hook for hanging pots above it, but these open fires were later
replaced by small enclosed ranges or 'kitcheners', with an oven and
water tank. There were numerous bakehouses in the town, often in
the cellars of corner shops, where you could take food to be baked, as

an aged Prestonian remembered in 1892, and these probably made up for the inadequacy of cooking facilities in many homes and the lack of time working wives had for cooking:

> In Paradise-street and Vauxhall-road were public bakehouses, for not much cooking was attended to at home. There was one also at the bottom of Pleasant-street. To these places bread and dinners were taken from the neighbourhoods.

Those houses where water was laid on had a single tap on the back wall of the wash-house, set over a shallow sink called a slopstone, perhaps with a draining board beside it. It was often directly connected to a drainpipe, a source of much woe, and was often contaminated by

The front room or living room of a Preston two-up, two-down house, complete with its 'kitchener' and a retired mill hand.

A Preston wash-house with its 'set-pot' in the corner towards the left.

sewage seeping out of the cesspit. When the privy contained a water-closet, it would share the drain, though this was unusual until much later in the century.

Another type of dwelling that was often thrown up to meet the growing need for accommodation was the 'back-to-back', although Preston did not as widely adopt these as some towns despite their inherent economies, and nor did Lancashire as a whole to the extent that, for example, neighbouring Yorkshire did. Even so, by the middle of the century there were about three hundred back-to-backs in Preston. The purpose of building the back-to-back house was to construct it as cheaply as possible by conserving both land and building materials to an even greater degree than in standard terrace houses. The back-to-back had only one wall facing outward, the other three being shared by neighbouring houses at each side and at the back. Usually it had only one room on each floor, though a second could be squeezed in to one side, and the stairs would probably rise in the gloom at the back. Each house generally had a living room with a bedroom over it, and perhaps another bedroom up a further flight of stairs. Some back-to-backs had a weaving cellar as well. It was difficult to provide enough light and ventilation for these rooms, but the real disadvantage compared with ordinary terrace houses was the lack of anywhere to put a privy. Usually an inadequate number of these were set up in blocks on any spare ground nearby. They were for all to share and none to clean.

Not every mill owner in the North was content to turn a blind eye to such living conditions; a few realised that disease was their enemy as well as that of their workers, and some even built model communities where standards were high and rents were low. Their aim was to attract and retain a moral, healthy and industrious workforce, rather than to produce the normal return on capital invested in housing, which was about 10 or 11 per cent. Because the rents they charged halved the return, it came to be known as 5 per cent philanthropy. Social obligation and economic advantage might nevertheless both be served. Thomas Ashton, for example, claimed that for every shilling he laid out in providing comfortable and respectable dwellings for his workers he received a very liberal interest in rent. Henry Ashworth, on the other hand, more typically made a return of only 5·2 per cent on his model estate at Turton near Bolton. His workers had suffered an outbreak of malignant fever made worse by the filthy and overcrowded state of their houses, so in the 1820s he had begun a programme of enlargement and improvement, providing a living room and back kitchen, both 15 feet by 9 feet, and three bedrooms.

These houses were very popular, although their weekly rent of 1s 6d was 6d more than it had been for the occupants' former houses. It was nevertheless a small amount for families bringing home 24s to 50s or even 60s per week. The houses were built to a high standard with kitchens that had sinks, boilers and ovens by their fireplaces. Every house had a private back yard with a privy, and, from 1835, piped water in the kitchen. The mill workers furnished the houses well with mahogany chests full of clothing, beds with sheets, blankets and quilts, and rooms with curtains and carpets. Thrift, Order, Promptitude and Perseverance formed the motto of the Ashworths, from which there was to be no shirking, but the reward was Prosperity and Respectability.

Akroyden, the model estate in the northern outskirts of Halifax, a monument to Edward Akroyd, one of the handful of benevolent mill owners.

Gradually the old nonconformist, evangelical conscience of people like the Ashworths, at war with vice, poverty, disease and a dozen other evils – above all, indifference, hardened as the nineteenth century wore on into a complacent moral code of respectability today and a stoic vision of progress tomorrow.

Such benevolent mill owners were not only inspired by the dream of an improved future. They also looked to the past. The two great Yorkshire mill owners and estate builders Edward Akroyd and Sir Titus Salt both believed that the old eighteenth-century rural paternalism could be transferred to industrial settlements. They were inspired by the romantic view of the squire and his tenants, all of them once sons of the soil together, now gently transformed to other tasks – 'bold peasants, rosy children, smoking joints, games on the green', as G M Young wrote: 'Merrie England, in a word, engaged in a flourishing export trade in coal and cotton'. Salt's biographer, R Balgarnie, recalled that he 'showed how the graces of the old feudalism . . . could be grafted on and exemplified by the men who brought forth and moulded the better age'. Akroyd shared this view. He was 'desirous of keeping up the old English notion of a village – the squire and the parson, as head and centre of all progress and good fellowship'. It was a hard-headed view too because, however good it was for the workers' morale, it also kept them amenable to the economic needs of the mills.

The conservative and yet progressive philosophy of the estates that Akroyd and Salt built – Copley, Akroyden and Saltaire – already had an influential literary expression in Disraeli's novel *Coningsby* of 1844. Close to Mr Millbank's factory in Lancashire was 'a village of not inconsiderable size, and remarkable from the neatness and even picturesque character of its architecture, and the gay gardens that surround it'. Further, it was a village complete with such social amenities as a church, school, and an institute with a library, lecture room, and reading room. In *Sybil*, Disraeli's next novel, comes the even more Utopian mill owner, Mr Trafford:

> Deeply had he pondered on the influence of the employer on the health and content of his workpeople. He knew well that the domestic virtues are dependent on the existence of a home, and one of his first efforts had been to build a village where every family might be well lodged.

But men of Akroyd's or Salt's vision were unusual. Preston and many other industrial towns had to rely on petty speculators to provide new housing, and the workers had to rest their hopes of better living conditions on something more diffuse and distant, reform by the state.

The wonder of the Victorian age was that it did set about reforming itself, the despair that it took so long. There were various factors which formed a brake on the reform of housing and everything else. For a start, the landed power of the rural eighteenth century did not quietly melt before the heat of the Age of Steam. If anything, it benefited from it. Land was increasingly in demand and brought more certain profit than the factory. Growing industry demanded sites for its machines and workers, and food to fuel their efforts. The mill owner, on the other hand, was less secure: he was always hunting for wider markets for his produce as its price fell. At the bottom of the heap, the mill workers too were always tightening their belts as those markets periodically disappointed expectations, and they were unable to afford as much food as they needed. Meanwhile, the privileges of the landowner, were reinforced by circumstance and the law alike.

Another brake on the improvement of housing was the widespread dislike of the state intervening in private matters. How people regulated their lives was for convention to decide. As the Tory statesman Edmund Burke had said, 'To these, great politicians may give a leaning, but they cannot give a law.'

Nevertheless, by the 1840s the sanguine figure of John Bull no longer represented the average Englishman. He was now factory fodder, pallid and broken-bodied. How many influential people, the Whig reformer Lord Morpeth asked Parliament, had ever

> 'tracked the swarm of human life, of decrepit age, of blighted manhood and of stunted infancy into the steaming and reeking receptacles of filth and fever, and every kind of loathsomeness, into which they are but too often stuffed and crammed'?

Outsiders feared the anarchy that might erupt from such slums, where, they felt, decent pride was extinguished and people were brought to a life of evident villainy, debauchery and licentiousness. Harsher minds, though, preferred to see the 'low' behaviour of the working classes as a cause, not a consequence, of the filth they lived in. But even though housing was a recognised scandal, its reform only came about through action taken by the government to improve health generally. This whole problem that so vexed Victorian reformers became known as the Sanitary Question. Such was its impact on the nation's mind that the Prussian historian and anglophobe Heinrich von Treitschke scathingly remarked, 'The English think soap is civilisation.'

Well they might. In 1832, cholera arrived in England from the East. It added to the number of water-borne diseases like typhus already endemic in crowded towns all over the country, and threatened not just the working classes but the ruling classes too. Overcrowding and the appalling state of urban sewers were clearly the cause, though the reasons why they were the cause were not understood. Many sewers were no more than foul-smelling ditches filled with everyone's stagnant excreta:

> dead dogs, cats, kittens, and rats; offal from slaughter-houses, sometimes even including the entrails of animals; street-pavement dirt of every variety; vegetable refuse; stable dung; the refuse of pig-styes; night-soil; ashes; tin kettles and pans.
>
> (J Robertson, Committee on Health of Towns, 1840)

A filthy cellar-dwelling, as depicted by Leech, inhabited not only by seven people, but also a donkey, a duck and a pair of rats fleeing from the rent collector.

It was not only the courts and cellars of Preston that squeezed themselves round such sewers, but all of Lancashire's.

Into this chaos came the figure of Edwin Chadwick, one of a small band of eager reformers known as the Utilitarians or Philosophical Radicals who took their lead from Jeremy Bentham. They challenged and indeed changed the philosophy of the times. Their belief was in progress, but a progress devoted to remedying the social evils of the day. Their method was to compile evidence, ideally through an official commission; this would pinpoint causes and prompt solutions which the government would impose by state intervention. The paternalism of a few benevolent mill owners was not enough. The state must act.

Chadwick was born in 1800 into a Lancashire farmhouse where the children were daily scrubbed all over. This profound influence prompted his life work. You could say he found England filthy and left it scrubbed – or would have done if only legislation had been more speedily effective. His public work began when the Manchester Statistical Society was compiling the first evidence of the deteriorating state of Lancashire's mill workers. In his thirties he joined and eventually led a Royal Commission to investigate the failings of the Poor Law, and reported to another Commission set up to consider the health of towns. He concluded that disease was ubiquitous because of 'atmospheric impurities produced by decomposing animal and vegetable substances, by damp and filth and close and overcrowded dwellings' – in fact by germs, though he was unable to name them. The remedy was clear; there had to be radical improvements in sanitation as he explained in his evidence to the Commission:

> where those circumstances are removed by drainage, proper cleansing, better ventilation and other means of diminishing atmospheric impurity, the frequency and intensity of such diseases is abated . . .

There would be clear advantages to the whole community from effective drainage, better water supplies and the removal of waste, but to achieve this there had to be proper organisation:

> for the protection of the labouring classes and of the rate payers against inefficiency and waste . . ., securities should be taken that all new local public works are devised and conducted by responsible officers.

It took a second outbreak of cholera to stir Parliament into action. In London alone 30000 cases were recorded in a population of 2·2 million, and about half were fatal. The nature of the disease was horrific: vomiting and diarrhoea leading to acute dehydration. At last it brought immediate legislation, the Public Health Act of 1848.

Sadly this Act was a compromise and had not the force of compulsion. Its intent was to improve the sanitary conditions of towns, and to do so it made several recommendations. Their supply of water, and their sewerage, drainage, cleansing and paving should become the responsibility of Local Boards of Health, a part of each town's newly reformed municipal authority. No new house should be built without drains nor without a privy containing either a water-closet or a cesspit. In future, builders should submit plans of their houses showing all these details to the local board for approval. The boards were to ensure that no further cellar dwellings were built and to control those already in use. They were to be responsible for the supply of water and other possible hazards to health such as burial grounds.

The Health Act was a major landmark in the improvement of working-class housing and a victory for reform. But it was by no means complete. The opposing forces of *laissez-faire* were not to be struck down at a blow and were quick to embrace a perverted interpretation of Darwin's theory of evolution of species, the survival of the fittest. *The Economist*, for example, was unable to offer the poor any more than a sanctimonious sniff:

> In our condition suffering and evil are nature's admonitions; they cannot be got rid of; and the impatient attempts of benevolence to banish them from the world by legislation, before benevolence has learnt their object and their end, have always been productive of more evil than good.   (13 May, 1848)

The poor obviously were to be killed either by kindness or by their poverty. They could not win.

The Act was in any case a compromise between what should be done and what those who would have to pay the bill were willing to accept. The Act only suggested rather than compelled, and there was much opposition – from town councils, developers and builders. (Often these were the same men, but wearing different hats.) It would mean higher costs, they said, and so higher rents, which the mass of tenants could not afford. Major improvement was consequently very slow in coming. Too much was left to local initiative because it was believed that individual towns understood their own problems best. This inevitably left them with much scope for inactivity.

So the Act had different consequences between one town and another. In Preston in 1850 the Town Council took on the responsibilities of a Local Board of Health. It faced a formidable problem as Nigel Morgan has shown in his *Housing in Victorian Preston* (1984). In cold statistics it counted 11500 dwellings occupied by nearly 70000 people, an average of six per dwelling. Many houses, of course, had far more. Forty years later in 1891 overcrowding was to be officially defined as more than two adults per room regardless of its size, children counting as halves and babies not at all. Even by these low standards, Preston's dwellings were still often overcrowded in 1891 and had been far more so in the 1840s. They ranged from single-roomed cellars to six-roomed houses. The better-paid families tended to occupy the larger houses and could live in some comfort, but they were not necessarily the larger families. Poorer people, on the other hand, could have hardly avoided overcrowding, such as the seventy-seven living in nine small dwellings in Turk's Head Yard.

The majority of people were housed in terraces of two-up, two-downs which had doubled and redoubled Preston's size in the 1830s

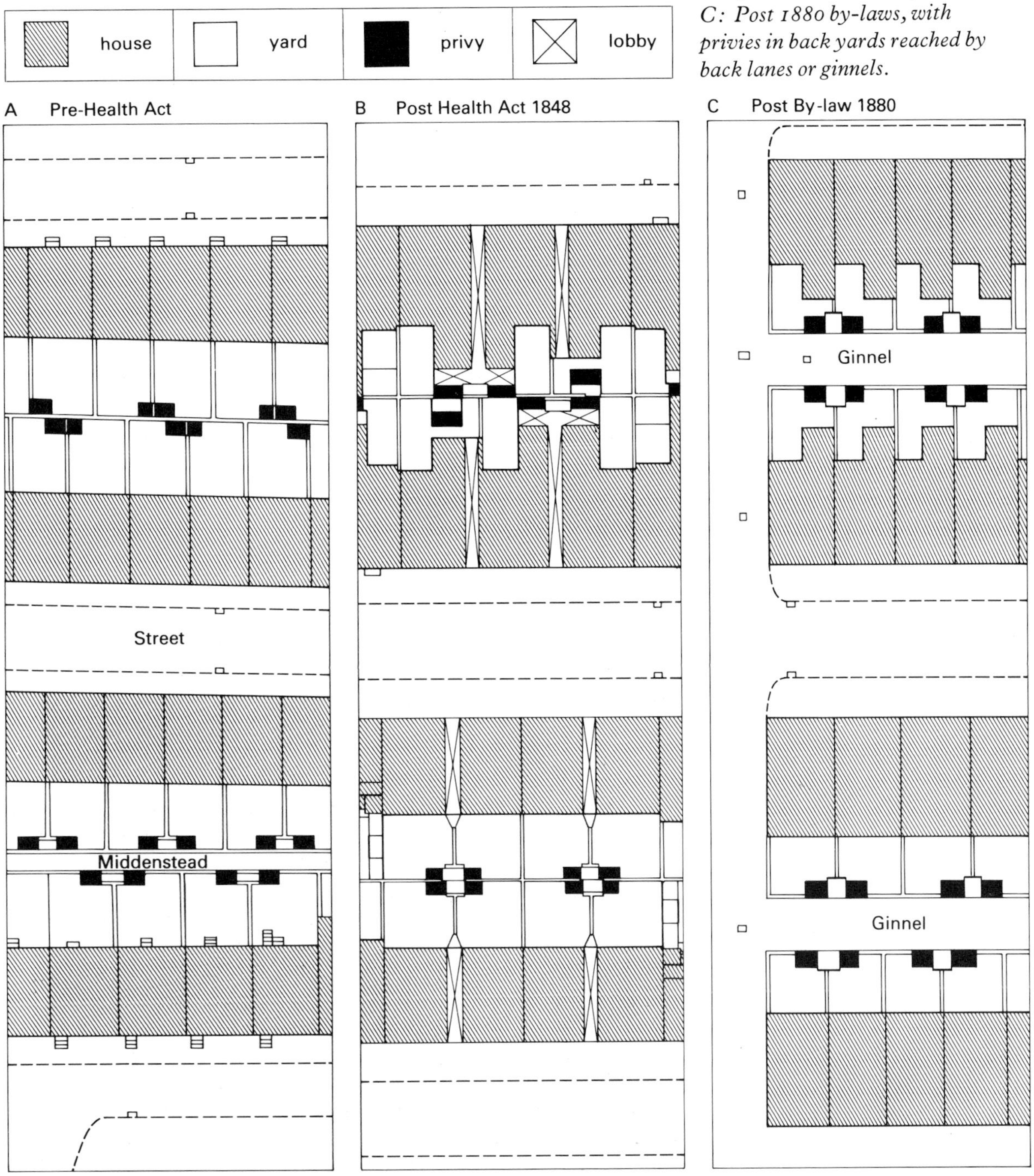

Three layouts of houses in Preston.

A: With privies in back yards, reached either through the houses (top), or by way of a middenstead (bottom).

B: Post 1848 Health Act, with privies reached by lobbies between every two houses leading to yards.

C: Post 1880 by-laws, with privies in back yards reached by back lanes or ginnels.

| house | yard | privy | lobby |

A   Pre-Health Act

Street

Middenstead

B   Post Health Act 1848

C   Post By-law 1880

Ginnel

Ginnel

and 1840s, and continued to do so right through the nineteenth century and up to the Great War. It was not so much with these houses that the Local Board of Health had to wrestle as with their privies. As the fields round the town became packed with streets and the streets with houses, so the back yards were reduced to a minimum. Since each yard contained a privy and its rubbish tip, or midden, this space restriction became crucial. The privy was a little hut 3 or 4 feet square built against the back wall of the yard and placed over a cesspit or occasionally over a drain leading to a communal cesspool, or, more rarely, to a sewer. The rubbish tip was placed alongside, as the ash thrown on it from the household fires was useful in covering the excreta in the privies and reducing the smell. From time to time scavengers were supposed to dig out the privies and remove the rubbish. The trouble was that there were only twelve men employed at this task in Preston, roughly one man for every thousand dwellings, and they were for the most part aged paupers unequal to the job. You were lucky if they came once every three months. Their job was not made any easier by the inaccessibility of many of the yards. Some could be reached only through the houses themselves, others only by

The arrangement of the back yards of houses in Preston can generally help to date them. Those shown here were probably built before the Public Health Act of 1848 took effect. The yards are cramped and the privies can only be reached by the scavengers through the dreadfully narrow middenstead that runs down the middle of the picture.

narrow alleys along the backs of the yards called middensteads, as the Board of Health inspector found in 1859:

> Between the backs of Stoney-gate and Library-street, is a narrow and very filthy passage, with an open gutter between two rows of open cesspools, clogged with accumulations of night soil. It seems to have been the plan, at one time, to build rows of cottages with this sort of narrow alley between them for the purposes of getting at their back premises. Such an alley, in Preston, is sure to be a receptacle for filth.

Many of Preston's population of mill workers were newly arrived from the countryside, and their rural activities made this problem stickier. Even as late as 1883 Dr Pilkington, Preston's Medical Officer of Health appointed by the Local Board, reported:

> There is a strong disposition on the part of many of the working classes to crowd up their already confined yards with pig-styes, hen roosts, and similar structures.

The livestock served the double purpose of consuming vegetable refuse and providing a welcome supplement to often thin diets, but they made a foul quagmire of the back yards.

Keeping animals in your yard was a fundamental contravention of the 1848 Public Health Act, but as the entire Act was only a recommendation, and needed by-laws to make it enforceable, this and other problems continued. Preston tried to get by without by-laws, even though the Local Government Act of 1858 gave the Council the power to pass them. It accepted the provisions of the Health Act so far as it stopped the building of back-to-backs and cellar dwellings, and continued with the airier, less crowded terraces of two-up, two-down houses with minimal back yards, but merely nodded in the direction of helping the scavengers do their job by making the builders provide slightly better access to the back yards than before. Instead of having to go through the houses, they could now reach pairs of yards by a separate passage that ran between every other house with its own doorway placed between the front doors of flanking houses.

These linked doorways give many of Preston's terraces their particular character, and they also served architectural propriety, as the doorways into the houses were larger, had fanlights over them and were decorated with pilasters or architraves, but the ones between them into the passages, or lobbies, as they came to be called, were left plain. They are a sure sign that the houses were originally built with back yards and privies, and that is how these houses remained for most of their lives. The lobbies led to pairs of yards, often of no more than 6 feet or so from the backs of the houses to their back walls. Not only might householders keep pigs in the yards, but they also found a novel use for the lobbies, as the Medical Officer of Health reported in 1883:

> In many cases, the covered lobby between the houses . . . is closed at one end, and converted into a fowl house, a pigeon cote, or even a stable.

Squalor often took your hand when you penetrated behind the lobby doors, and it started with the poor means of removing the excrement.

Back yards in Preston after the Public Health Act took effect. The yards are larger and now reached, pair by pair, from the street by way of lobbies, one appearing to the left of the modern drain pipe together with the gateway to the yard. The privy, built against the wall in the foreground, is just out of view to the extreme left.

The promoters of the Public Health Act had pressed for water-closets to be installed in yards, but the Act recognised that there would be difficulties in enforcing this and allowed cesspits as an alternative. In any case Preston had to continue using cesspits in the first instance simply because there was not the water to do otherwise. In the 1840s Preston Waterworks was supplying half of Preston's houses; that is to say, some 5000 houses had a tap each and, provided water was used sparingly, it would flow when the tap was turned on. But there was nothing like enough to supply water-closets, and even the new reservoir constructed in the 1850s still did not provide enough. Neither were there the sewers to carry off effluent. Between 1851 and 1881 the population of Preston increased by some 40 per cent while the number of houses rose by 80 per cent. This provided an average of one house for every four and a half persons rather than for the six of 1851, so overcrowding had been significantly reduced. But although sewers were at last completed in 1865 after fifteen years of dispute and hard work, the water supply was still a problem and Preston remained a town of privies. It expanded faster than these services could catch up.

One service which Preston did have was gas. There were gas works in Preston well before the middle of the nineteenth century, but mill workers' houses were not connected to the supply until much later. At first their houses were lit in the age-old way by oil lamps and candles. This must have added to the hardships of life, especially in autumn and winter when all the daylight hours were spent at the mill.

None of these houses had front gardens, and the entrances into the living-rooms opened directly out to the street. As a result, the streets became communal meeting places. However filthy your back yard might

be, you scrubbed your front doorstep for public show and pride in the home. It was also a place for endless conversation with your neighbours, and the street itself gave you a sense of communal identity from the time you started to play in it as a child until your neighbours said farewell to you when the cart took your coffin to the cemetery. The authorities frowned on all this: streets were thoroughfares, not places for what they suspected might possibly be subversive activities.

The new streets built by the speculators in Preston were laid out as a grid, acre by acre, and filled with houses. On the north side of Preston, for example, was a patch of wasteland. It went by the grand title of the Moor Hall Estate, though when it had been built up it was called Plungington. In 1855 it was bought for development by Thomas and William Tomlinson, who employed the local architect and surveyor John James Myres, incidentally a member of the Local Board of Health, and a useful man to cut bureaucratic corners. He laid out a rectangular pattern of streets, 72 feet apart, then divided the land into building blocks which he sold off to small builders. They had to pay ground rent to the Tomlinsons and build houses specified in their agreements. These could not be back-to-backs nor contain cellar dwellings (so far had the Public Health Act been effective) and, according to the building agreements, must be

> at least eighteen feet high from the Threshold to the square [eaves], and shall not comprise . . . more than two stories, and shall be at least fifteen feet in width in front . . .

The builders and, indeed, other tradesmen looking for a small investment, then endeavoured to obtain a mortgage on their newly acquired

Life in Cranbourne Street, off New Hall Lane, Preston, in about 1927. A fishmonger with his cart is apparently adjusting an oil lamp, probably because he also sold paraffin. The houses in this street had hallways and parlours, with wash-houses in their tunnel-backs.

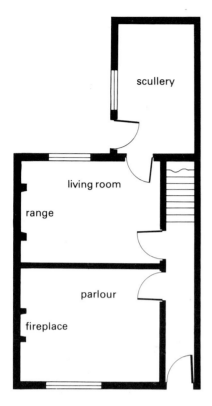

Plan of a tunnel-back showing how the provision of an extension for the scullery allows space for a parlour at the front. Most tunnel-backs had a third bedroom over the scullery.

sites so they could start to build. Their houses 'at least fifteen feet in width' were usually exactly 15 feet in width, and their plots took half the 72 feet between the streets – that is to say, 36 feet for house and yard. The houses were built directly on to the street with a front room, more or less 15 feet square, a rear room, about 10 feet deep, and a yard, again about 10 feet deep, taking up the remaining space. The lobby that ran between the houses took about 3 feet from the double plot, and what lay above was given to one house (instead of being divided between the two) so it had wider bedrooms.

Though some had rotten foundations, poor bricks and flimsy roofs, in general these houses were not badly built, their fronts not unattractive individually. The streets, on the other hand, seem endless to strangers: Barlow Street, Hammond Street, Miles Street, Havelock Street, Villiers Street. . . .

Despite first impressions the houses were not all exactly the same and numerous little differences gave them a measure of individuality. Some, for example, had a rear extension. It might be no larger than a small lean-to with a tap and sink, but some were large enough to contain a fully fledged wash-house with a third bedroom over it. A terrace house with a large extension like this was called a tunnel-back. It had the disadvantage of taking most of the space from the back yard and making it darker and more airless than ever. Nevertheless the extra rooms made all the difference to a house's accommodation.

A quarter of the houses in Plungington were tunnel-backs. With the wash-house now in the extension, the back room in the body of the house could become a general living and cooking room, and the front room a parlour. With three bedrooms above, there was less need for anyone to sleep downstairs. These tunnel-backs were usually a little wider than two-up, two-downs, and so had a narrow internal passage from the front door to the rear and the stairs. This made the rooms that opened off it completely private – essential for a parlour.

To have a parlour was the height of ambition not just among Preston's mill workers, but among working-class families everywhere. As the nineteenth century progressed, the parlour became an almost sacred shrine to family life, even in the most crowded households. It was sacrosanct. When cottage industry was a family affair, a parlour was an ordinary private room, but now that mills and other centres of employment took all the members of the family outside the house for so much of their lives, they needed a tangible symbol of their unity and success. So it came about that they scrimped and saved to decorate their parlours with symbols of their meagre wealth, often bought on hire purchase. A cheap, varnished dining suite of table, chairs and sideboard or dresser became the scene of formal Sunday midday dinners. An equally cheap upright piano brought the family together to sing sentimental ballads like *The Miner's Dream of Home*. The mantelpiece, a glass-fronted cabinet with shelves, and all the other horizontal surfaces were covered with carefully placed curios bought on holiday excursions. Eventually they were joined by family photographs, the ultimate demonstration of the family's existence, just like the oil paintings of the rich.

Here in the parlour the family went through the formal occasions of life, such as entertaining relatives, celebrating weddings, laying out

A back lane, or ginnel, at last made compulsory in Preston following the passing of by-laws in 1880. The house in the foreground is a tunnel-back and so had three rooms to each storey and could therefore have included a parlour.

A parlour at the turn of the century complete with piano and photographs. The music – When the Boys Come Home *– probably refers to the Boer War.*

and mourning the dead, and above all, eating the one leisurely meal of the week. But, come Monday, it would be deserted, the carpet swept, the grate emptied and blacked, the brass polished, the blinds drawn down to stop the carpet fading, and the door closed until next Sunday. Today these parlours, replete with the symbols rather than the substance of family life, seem to typify the stifling respectability of the times. In fact they set the scene for much joy.

In contrast the back room, the living-room, was full of bustling life, of cooking and eating, bathing in the tub before the fire, and playing when it was wet. It was where friends would drop in for a chat. It was full of all the everyday household goods. Even the coal had to be dumped under the stairs if you did not have a cellar.

Such houses were filled with cotton workers and many others in all the trades and professions that supported them. In 1871 there were 1600 people in Plungington living in 321 houses. Although that produces an average of five per house, numbers typically varied from two to twelve and more. No. 8 Hammond Street had twelve occupants, a married couple and eight adult sons and daughters, one of them with his wife, another widowed and with a child. The house had an extension and three bedrooms, but how everyone packed into bed is hard to guess. Even so the house would not have been officially designated as overcrowded by the later definition of 1891.

Overcrowded or not, it would nevertheless have promoted disease. In part this depended on the occupants and their knowledge of hygiene, as Preston's Medical Officer of Health noted in 1896. There were many well scrubbed households, but in others dirt reigned supreme, he reported:

> The food to be consumed is left lying about in contact with dirty clothes and unwashed cooking utensils. In the bedrooms the windows are left unopened, the slops unemptied, and the beds unmade, until the chamber is again required for the night. Pigeons create dirt and breed vermin upstairs or in the cellars, while wretched fowls scratch amongst the refuse and excrement in the ashpit, and afterwards come indoors to shake the foul germ-laden dust from their feathers over the already contaminated food. The children are unwashed and uncombed, and – saddest sight of all – not unfrequently in a dirty cradle they may be seen a sour-smelling baby sucking at a still more evil-smelling feeding bottle.

Germs were now at last recognised for what they were. Even so in these houses they exploited the many opportunities they had to strike. Two statistics make this clear. In terms of plain mortality Preston was unhealthy and getting unhealthier as the nineteenth century progressed. Each year in the 1840s an average of twenty-eight people in a thousand died. By the 1850s the number was over thirty and by the early 1870s had risen to 30·26. By then it was clear, as James Hibbert told his colleagues on the Town Council in 1875, that 'the rate of mortality is higher in the closely packed, newly erected dwellings' of neighbourhoods like Plungington. In England generally mortality was far lower, and between 1851 and 1881 actually fell from 21·8 to 19·7. Today it is about twelve. Even in industrial Lancashire as a whole it was well below Preston's. More shocking than this was the infant mortality rate. Preston's was a third higher than the average for large towns and worse than in any other Lancashire town. Over one baby in five in the last two decades of the nineteenth century never reached the age of one, and in the saddest years more than one died in four. Despite the advances in medical science, these figures seem to be worse than those of the ignorant seventeenth century.

So why was Preston's health record apparently so poor? In part this can be explained by the fact that workers' housing in Preston was so evenly spread. There was no salubrious and healthy quarter in the town to reduce the overall impact of the statistics. Preston was in fact showing the worst face of Lancashire, where other towns could hide theirs behind the veil of well-to-do suburbs.

The front entrance of two houses in Wellfield Road, Preston, with the entrance to the lobby between them. These houses were scheduled for demolition because they were so cramped, but were still occupied in 1984.

The fronts of tunnel-back houses built in 1852 in Nelson Terrace, Preston. Despite their six rooms, the houses were so small and their back yards so cramped that they have had to be scheduled for demolition. The nearest house (on the left) is at the end of the terrace, and its yard can be reached from the side, but further down the street the yards are reached by lobbies, so there is the characteristic third doorway between the decorated front doors.

A ginnel between the back yards of rows of houses off St Stephen's Road, Preston, built soon after the by-laws of 1880 took effect.

At first infant mortality was widely but wrongly blamed on the mothers. It was claimed they packed their child-bearing into too short a period so as to get back to the mill and their wage packets. But though no doubt some women were poor mothers and their abilities as housewives inadequate, in Preston they were presented with a problem that no amount of love and care could solve. Their babies were dying from infantile diarrhoea, and the reason soon became clear. In 1883 the Medical Officer of Health, Dr Pilkington, was able to assert:

> The conditions in which infantile diarrhoea prevails are those in which the middensteads, occupying a portion of the limited yard space, are often in close proximity to the dwellings themselves . . . where the pavement in the yard is defective and becomes soaked with slop-water and other liquid refuse, and where as a result the summer's sun instead of bringing health and pleasure becomes a generator of evil odours and of dangerous gases.

Scavengers at work removing the night soil, 1849.

The stark reality was that Preston's housing was as great a hazard to health in 1900 as it had been in 1850, despite the recommendations of the Public Health Act, the reforming work of the Local Board of Health, and even the eventual introduction of local by-laws to promote better health. It gave the impression that those who had opposed the measures had been right; reform had apparently produced more evil than good. The advocates of self-interested *laissez-faire* said as much, like this 'Prestonian' in a letter to the *Preston Chronicle* on 22 March, 1862:

> . . . a code of by-laws has been in progress of hatching, with a python-sort of eagerness, for some years past, fruitlessly as well as needlessly. The town stands in danger of one of the greatest evils that can befall it, to stop its growth, to damage the interests of investors, to check, control and annoy the building business, to terrify the ignorant workman, to strike the intolerant glance of power at every sort of individual at all interested or desirous to see Preston pursue its destiny of a thriving, healthy, and model manufacturing town.

While other towns had brought in by-laws and built much improved houses, Preston had resisted. Reform never had a chance. Always the builders and landowners had effectively been able to block it. When, for example, by-laws were proposed in 1862 to counter jerry-building, to insist on basic standards for drains, and a minimum size of 150 square feet for back yards, a builder wrote to the *Preston Chronicle* (29 March, 1862) to say 'They seem more like the laws of Russia than English laws'. Perhaps there was the shred of an excuse for such a reaction in 1862; that was a difficult year. Civil war in the United States had brought cotton famine to Lancashire and the hardship lasted until 1864. But in both the decade before and the decade afterwards trade had been booming. In truth, it was not lack of money that stopped reform but obstinate self-interest. Other towns were willing to invest in improvements and pass by-laws, but not Preston.

When Gladstone's Public Health Act of 1872 made the appointment of a Medical Officer of Health by Preston Town Council mandatory, the opposition effectively delayed the appointment for two years and then refused to employ him on more than a half-time basis. When the death rate reached a monstrous thirty-nine per thousand in 1874, J J Myres, the architect and surveyor of Plungington, turned the evidence upside down and said that Preston was improving. It was just a chance epidemic of smallpox, scarlatina and measles that made the statistics seem so bad, Myers declared to the Council, and it was the fault of the inhabitants that they fell ill:

> Preston was a most healthy town; but it was their own filthiness, and their own carelessness, and recklessness that had brought them into such a state.

Naturally, neither he nor the rest of the opposition led by such men as his employer, William Tomlinson, were going to lay the blame on the houses from which they had profited. Had they not spent – wasted – £50000 on sewerage, and it had made no difference?

Nevertheless a Medical Officer of Health, Dr H O Pilkington, was at last appointed in 1874, and he methodically demonstrated how disease and the inadequacies of the town's housing were related. The terrible mortality of infants, he showed, was a consequence of the drains into which slopstones and water-closets were directly connected, so allowing germ-laden gases to be fed straight back into the houses and their back yards. He and his allies on the Town Council promoted new by-laws requiring sewers to be properly ventilated and all connections to be trapped to stop germ-laden air flowing into the houses. In addition, as the Council heard, the yards themselves were far too small.

> . . . the spaces are so confined and crowded with buildings as to prevent the free circulation of air. . . . You have nothing but a series of stagnant wells of impure air – air that is rendered still fouler by emanations from badly-constructed and unfrequently-emptied middensteads and which . . . the people who inhabit these dwellings must breathe.

New by-laws were framed to remedy this as well. The answer, it was felt, lay in back lanes, locally called ginnels:

> . . . to provide facilities for frequent scavenging, by day as well as by night, and also to secure a sufficient distance apart of the parallel rows of buildings . . . back streets . . . should be compulsory. . . .

The back lanes were to be 12 feet wide, the back yards a minimum size of 240 square feet, even though this was less than neighbouring Blackburn's by no means generous standard of 270 square feet.

One of the proposers of this by-law, Councillor James Hibbert, stressed the link between mortality and the lack of space. No one, he asserted at a Council meeting, had a right to build on his land:

> in such a manner as may be detrimental to the health of the inhabitants. In short, the object we wish to secure is . . . 'The greatest happiness or good of the greatest number.' . . . Although landowners and speculative builders are entitled to their due share of consideration, yet their number is infinitesimally small compared with the labouring population, whose interests we are here to guard. They cannot help themselves. They must . . . live in such dwellings as are provided for them.

Tomlinson again opposed the measure, raising the old objection of increased rents, and another critic wrote to the press condemning back lanes for being prey to filth, and worse.

> They are simply harbours for vagabonds, gossips, burglars and other bad characters. No one can feel their house safe with such nuisances behind them.

They managed to emasculate the by-laws so that when they were finally confirmed in 1876 their effect was negligible. Bigger back yards were made compulsory, but back lanes or ginnels were not required. It took a new set of by-laws passed only in 1880 to make back lanes compulsory. Foreseeing then that the tide was at last turning against them, builders and land-owners, Tomlinson among them, made sure that all their future plans were approved before the Act became law, and so were able to continue to build without providing lanes for many years more.

Even so there were several improvements in both the houses and streets after these by-laws were passed. A walk down Charnock Road towards St Stephen's Road shows them clearly. Suddenly the street broadens. No longer do the terraces have three doorways in a row. It is one house, one door, and behind all the houses are the back lanes that Pilkington and Hibbert fought Myres and Tomlinson so hard to obtain. The houses are better built too, with good foundations and higher rooms. Many are tunnel-backs and so have two extra rooms as well.

These houses are now treasured, where the older, smaller, more densely packed houses have often had to be declared unfit for habitation and demolished. But was it so famous a victory? The people who first occupied these improved houses with their higher ceilings and back lane access in conformity with the 1880 by-laws had not even been born when the Public Health Act of 1848 was passed. It was a depressingly long time after the Act that they began to appear, an extreme case of local influence resisting change. Further, one of the improvements that Pilkington and Hibbert strove for, the back lanes, were only needed because privies with cesspits that had to be emptied, rather than water-closets flushing into a main drain, were still the norm. Between 1875 and 1888 the number of cesspits rose from nearly 13000 to 20000. Only in the 1890s did their numbers start to fall, until by 1900 perhaps half the houses counted a water-closet among their amenities and the mortality rate at last started falling.

By then Myres and Tomlinson had long since had their reward, the decades of building what they wanted to build with little restriction. In fact Tomlinson did better. In 1882 he was elected MP for Preston in the Conservative interest and remained so for nearly thirty years. Before his time was up he was Sir William Edward Murray Tomlinson, Bart, JP, DL. Obviously it pays to be a land-owner.

Tomlinson's tenants and constituents on the other hand had a different reward. By the standards of England at large, inordinate numbers of them, above all the babies, got where they were by a different kind of box, not the ballot box, but one that came to take them from their homes, especially when the weather was hot and the overpowering smell of the foetid back yards drifted through the houses, out of the lobbies and ginnels, and assailed you in the street.

CHAPTER SIX
Cottages for All

From the new vantage point of their aeroplanes, the aviators of the first decades of this century saw the towns and cities of a densely populated England spread below them like a map. They could pick out the tight knot of streets and buildings in ancient town centres, the radiating thoroughfares and ribbons of houses that lined them, and the ordered streets of packed terraces that filled the gaps between. If they looked carefully at the fringes of some towns they could see a new pattern. This was to be the pattern of the future. It lacked the familiar, age-old web of interconnecting streets, and instead had all the confusing appearance of a maze. The streets twisted and turned, continually branching out into fresh streets. Some rapidly turned back on themselves; others came to an abrupt halt. All over the place, little groups of houses straggled around these contortions in a curious counterpoint. The military precision one could see in the grid of streets and terraces marching in step as in Preston and most industrial towns was quite missing. This new, maze-like pattern, nevertheless, was not entirely formless. If the aviators flew high enough to get an overall view they could see a peculiar order in it, as though they were looking at a living organism under a microscope.

Groups of cottages nudged their way along the streets. Trees and greens filled in the gaps where cottages stood back from the roads, and there were gardens everywhere. The designers of these new homes would have liked you to think a time-machine had taken you back a few centuries to a brand-new village in an imaginary golden past before the evils of industrial towns had blighted life and scarred the land.

This is, in fact, exactly how these new estates of houses were conceived. Their designers could not turn back the clock, but they did want to remove the legacy of bad housing that the Industrial Revolution had heaped on the shoulders of the working classes. Indeed, a stroll down Fitzneal Street in East Acton, to take an example in London, does take you into a different world. It is a long way from the factory and its hordes of workers, both in appearance and actual distance.

Yet the seemingly age-old, artless quality of the houses and the happy accident of their setting are highly contrived. They are the work of architects and the first generation of planners, who were now closely involved in housing in a large way. This was a significant difference from the past. These architects were fully conversant with the latest styles, and they lived for a vision, which was to make it possible for working families to exchange the drabness of densely built-up towns for open, leafy surroundings that would bring a healthy glow to their cheeks. Out of this vision came a wholly new environment.

The strange thing about this environment is how traditional it looks. You can see this in numerous estates in outer London and nowhere better than at East Acton in the London borough of Hammersmith.

Around a curve of the Central Line of the Underground railway there is a little patch of winding streets and clusters of picturesque cottages. This is the Old Oak estate, one of the great pioneering works of the London County Council; it takes its romantic name from the nearby Old Oak Common. Built between 1911 and 1914 and continued after the Great War it is the culmination of the LCC architects' aesthetic ideas about housing the working classes.

Only recently had local authorities started to build at all. It was even more of an innovation that a local authority with responsibility for the immense metropolis, and consequently saddled with a commensurate burden of poor housing and destitution, should be trying to find a remedy for this in building little villagey groups of cottages. It seems an impractically small-scaled solution to a huge problem.

That was not so. The Council's architects were fully aware of their duty to house the masses, and took it up with crusading zeal. It may seem strange that they should have turned their backs on *all* the characteristics of urban building, not just the worst ones, in their search for a solution to the chronic problem of overcrowding, but they had espoused an ideal and were not looking for ordinary solutions. They saw themselves as designing for individual people, however large their numbers, not the faceless masses. They therefore aimed to reconcile the needs of towns with what they saw as the best qualities of villages, especially their individuality, airiness and natural beauty. So they came to build garden suburbs.

They were pressed into building suburbs at all because of the sheer intractability of the problem of the inner city. Preston, with its laggardly record, demonstrated the difficulties that public-spirited officials had had in wrenching the smallest amount of decency from the forces of *laissez-faire*. London, by contrast, neither lacked public-spirited reformers nor numbers of benevolent bodies all trying to raise the living conditions of the poor. They sponsored various kinds of model dwellings from terraces of houses to tenement blocks. Nonetheless, these hardly dented the housing problem. New roads, docks and railways were continually being driven through slums, leaving their inhabitants to crowd into whatever other accommodation they could find, which usually caused fresh slums to develop.

The Old Oak estate: a brand-new village in an imaginary golden past.

There was one problem that London did solve. In 1851, the year when the Great Exhibition demonstrated Britain's artistic, scientific and industrial achievements to the world, London was drowning in its own sewage and paying the price in disease. This ghastly penalty of uncontrolled expansion had caused concern for years. At last, in 1856, the Metropolitan Board of Works was called into being and charged with finding a solution. By the late 1860s the board had completed a sewerage system that was the envy of the world.

The Metropolitan Board of Works initiated the firm, organised control that took on some of the burden of what was then the world's largest city. The Industrial Revolution and the expansion of commerce that went with it had so enlarged London that it outdistanced ancient Rome as the greatest city that Europe had ever known. Wordsworth was horrified by the new industrial towns that had grown up at the same time, but he eulogised London.

Earth has not anything to show more fair . . .

From the safe distance of Westminster Bridge he gloried in London's monuments:

Ships, towers, domes, theatres, and temples lie
Open unto the fields, and to the sky . . .
(*On Westminster Bridge*)

Had he looked closer, though, even right by the hallowed ground of Westminster Abbey, he would have seen the Devil's Acre, a slum as satanic as any of those in Preston. Years after London's modernised sewerage system was inaugurated, London was still blighted by its slums and the toll of overcrowding. Today's smart theatreland round Drury Lane was so foul in the 1870s that death annually took forty people from every thousand who lived there, nearly double the average mortality rate. Much of the East End was just as bad.

The response to this was not supine inactivity, but all kinds of building programmes. For a start there were several philanthropic institutions. The Society for Improving the Conditions of the Labouring Classes, the Metropolitan Association for Improving the Dwellings

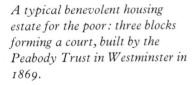

A typical benevolent housing estate for the poor: three blocks forming a court, built by the Peabody Trust in Westminster in 1869.

of the Industrious Classes, the Artisans', Labourers' and General Dwellings' Company, the Peabody Trust and many others all offered remedies. They built a variety of decent but basic dwellings that usually contained two or three bedrooms and a living–cooking room. Sculleries, bathrooms and even water-closets were often shared. The hope was that these new dwellings would make it possible to remove the poor from their sordid, run-down slums, but unfortunately there were not nearly enough new dwellings to solve the problem. They had a secondary aim, which was to set an example for others to follow, but that was optimistic. The kind of rents that the poor could pay did not even bring a glint to the eye of the urban landowners, speculators and builders whom the philanthropists hoped would follow suit.

There was no immediate official response, either. It too was hampered, but not by the need to make a profit. The Metropolitan Board of Works had no legal powers to build houses and this was a serious impediment. The only direct action it could take to improve housing conditions was to clear slums, and then to auction the land to prospective builders on the condition that they rehoused the poor displaced by the clearance.

Valiantly the Board of Works strove to eradicate the slums near Drury Lane in this way. In 1879 it purchased a site between Drury Lane, Kemble Street and Wild Street at a cost of £120000, and cleared it. This done, the Board resold the land to the Peabody Trust for just under £16000, and at the same time passed on the problem of rehousing the displaced slum dwellers. There were nearly 2000 of these poor people, of whom 240 would have to share a common lodging-house. Even so, the task was impossible and the Trust could squeeze in only 1620 of them. So more than 300 lost what poor homes they had had, and the rest were accommodated in a vast, six-storeyed block built round a tightly enclosed court.

Edwardian England had 4000 or 5000 of these blocks set over the cleared slums of London and other large towns. Many of them provided comparatively good homes, but often they looked dark and barrack-like. 'Pass by in the night,' wrote the Victorian novelist George Gissing in *The Nether World*,

> and strain the imagination to picture the weltering mass of human weariness, of bestiality, of unmerited dolour, of hopeless hope, of crushed surrender, tumbled together within those forbidding walls.

England did strain its imagination, and did not like the picture.

Gissing wrote these gloomy words in 1889. In that same year the LCC was formed from the Metropolitan Board of Works and other local government boards. This had greater authority and greater powers, and in 1890 was enabled by the Housing of the Working Classes Act to build houses on its own account. In 1893, the LCC's Architects Department formed a new group called the Housing of the Working Classes Branch. Its architects set themselves to building large blocks of dwellings in the place of cleared slums. Increasingly, they humanised the scale and appearance of these blocks through their layout and architecture. They avoided a regimented arrangement of the individual blocks, and made their appearance less massive and overbearing by cleverly varying the elevations and decoration.

Providence Place, Stepney, photographed at the beginning of this century. It was far from being the worst of London's slums but it shows how large numbers of people were crowded into closely spaced houses of the smallest size.

A group photograph of children in Treadwell Street, Shoreditch, some of whom moved to the White Hart Lane estate.

The first areas they tackled were in Bethnal Green and then in Westminster where they replaced bad slums with buildings in this new enlightened style. Nevertheless, just as the Metropolitan Board of Works had found, you could not remove a slum and still keep all its occupants on the same site. Part III of the 1890 Housing Act pointed to a remedy; it enabled local authorities to go further than simply replacing slum property by clearing it and building new, improved dwellings. Now they were allowed to buy land and provide housing elsewhere for people made homeless by slum clearances. Moreover, they could tackle the wider problem of housing shortages with their building programmes as well as the localised problem of slums.

In the election of 1898 the Progressive Party came to power in the LCC. This alliance of Liberal and Fabian reformers resolved to use Part III of the Housing Act to the full. They saw it not simply as a means of providing housing for people displaced by the clearances of slums like the 'Old Nichol' in Bethnal Green and Millbank in Westminster, but as a means of reducing overcrowding everywhere.

This, then, is how the new suburban estates of cottages came into being. Because there could be no complete solution to overcrowding in the centre of town simply by exchanging slums for blocks of new dwellings, an alternative had to be sought elsewhere. The fringes of London seemed to offer the best solution. Land values were lower there than in the centre. In some respects they were markedly lower because there was no competition from agriculture, which had been in the doldrums since cheap imports of food from the 1880s had ruined its profitability. Furthermore, the new railways and tramways had made the suburbs much more accessible, and cheap early-morning workers' tickets allowed at least the better paid of the capital's labour force to commute long distances. The old relationship between where you lived and where you worked could now be eroded.

No one in control greatly regretted this change. The docks and markets and workshops of the East End were widely held to manufacture equal measures of filth, disease and vice. The appeal of the new, bright suburbs would be strong, the reformers believed, and the hours of travel and cheap tickets a small price to pay for a salubrious home.

In this context the architects of the Housing Branch started to extend the principles that had already inspired their first blocks of dwellings in Bethnal Green and Millbank. In the outer areas they were able to have more freedom in the design of their estates of cottages, because land was cheaper and they did not need to accommodate so many people or so many dwellings to the acre. Furthermore, designing cottages allowed more flexibility than laying out blocks of dwellings. There were, of course, constraints. For example, financial considerations put a limit on the size of their new cottages because there had to be a return on capital investment via the rent that could be charged. Nevertheless, a two-bedroomed cottage usually had rather more floor space than its equivalent in a block of dwellings (though this was not much), all the cottages had their own sculleries and water-closets (these had often been shared in the blocks of dwellings) and about half of them were additionally to have bathrooms. This meant that the architects had to exercise much ingenuity in planning the cottages, but they had more scope for creative imagination than they had had in their blocks of dwellings, and could lean on an immeasurably longer tradition of building. They rose to the challenge with enthusiasm.

The practice of building model cottages can be traced back to the Middle Ages, and was particularly popular among the rural landowners of the eighteenth and nineteenth centuries. They sought to improve the picturesque qualities of their estates and at the same time to provide their tenants with better houses and their coffers with increased rents. Old cottages tumbled, and sometimes whole villages were swept away if they spoiled the view from a stately home. In their place came new groups of model houses, sometimes complete villages of them, in a multitude of fashionable styles. Harewood in North Yorkshire was classical, and the cottages of Edensor near Chatsworth in Derbyshire were in every style you can think of – Italianate, castellated, Gothic, Norman, Swiss chalet and so on. Most importantly for the future, Blaise Hamlet near Bristol was in a rustic style, though so quaintly exaggerated that its little group of cottages remains a great joke to this day. You half expect caricatures of country yokels to live there in smocks and floppy hats and clumping boots.

Blaise Hamlet was started in 1811. Fifty years later its style had been overlain by all the earnestness that the Gothic revival could give it. Romantic but fervent writers like Augustus Welby Pugin and then John Ruskin promoted the revival of the medieval Gothic style with the conviction of moral certainty. They believed it was the epitome of Christian piety and a supposed medieval morality, and that no other style could be contemplated by a Christian country like Victorian England. By the 1860s most leading architects had come to agree that Gothic was the essential style for a Christian church, but they were also coming to realise that it was generally too emphatic for a small house. An easy application of the rustic features of earlier vernacular houses was thought more suitable, and so the Old English style came

Old England as re-created at Blaise Hamlet in 1811.

into being. It did not have quite the moral certainty of the Gothic style, but it did exemplify to them a kind of Christian morality by recalling a time when Christian craftsmen could inspire their work with the moral worth of their own powers of creation. It would be enough, they felt, to produce a good effect on all who came into contact with such houses. The variety of the style, as well as its details, were thought to be an appropriate denial of the boring uniformity of the classical style, which, Pugin recalled, had originated at a time when people worshipped pagan gods. Less appropriately to the Victorian age, the Old English style implied a denial of the methods of mass production that the Industrial Revolution was increasingly bringing to the building trades.

Many of the architects working in the Old English style supported the Arts and Crafts Movement. This wide group of aesthetically minded men and women believed that architecture, and indeed life itself, were fields in which the foremost workers in each art and craft should unite in doing their best. Their prophet, William Morris, was like a breath of fresh air in late Victorian England. He offered a way out of the miseries of industrialised England through his Utopian vision of a society at once devoted to a socialist egalitarianism and to individual endeavour. He devoted his creative energies to wallpaper, textiles and furniture, and set up a firm to manufacture them by hand in the old way. Through these products he touched all the visual arts, and through his writings, a whole age.

The simplicity, clarity and economy of Morris's designs were sorely needed for the times he lived in were too easily tempted by opulent grandeur. The simplicity and clarity were also of the greatest importance to the development of a modern aesthetic in the twentieth century. Yet modernists believe that Morris and the Arts and Crafts Movement failed at the last jump: they could not reconcile themselves to the machine. That was the legacy of an ill-founded romantic belief in the moral superiority of the Middle Ages. Our present, wider view is more lenient. We are painfully aware that the whole-hearted acceptance of the machine ethic in architecture has brought the acute problems of industrialised, prefabricated, system-built dwellings. There has not been the liberation from the housing problem that the protagonists of modern architecture expected. Meanwhile, we recognise William Morris, romantic visionary that he was, as a supreme designer. The unresolved dilemma in his beliefs, essentially the conflict between the needs of the individual and the needs of the densely packed masses of urban society, is still with us and probably always will be.

Morris's vision of Old England influenced the first garden suburb, Bedford Park in West London, which was started in 1875. Its leafy streets of cosy, red-brick houses with their gables and tile-hanging are the epitome of the Old English style. Morris approved, and thought it was all 'quaint and pretty', but its arty character was too much for the sceptical. For them Bedford Park was a place 'Where men may lead a chaste correct Aesthetical existence'.

However you view Bedford Park, such an existence was poles apart from the reputedly vicious, loose, boorish existence of slum dwellers. So when the LCC's Housing Branch architects started to design suburban estates they remembered Bedford Park and how Morris had written in

A place to lead a 'chaste correct Aesthetical existence': Bedford Park's houses in the 'Old English' style.

Art and Beauty of the Earth of the necessity of changing England 'from the grimy back yard of a workshop into a garden'. In the 1890s the design of the LCC's few small cottage estates progressively moved away from the plain uniformity of the unadorned terrace towards a more varied grouping of houses in short rows. This trend was accentuated in the larger estates that followed the turn of the century.

In the first two of them, the Totterdown Fields estate at Tooting and the first phase of the White Hart Lane estate at Tottenham, the streets followed the old grid pattern common throughout the nineteenth century, but its endlessness was reduced by slight changes in the alignment of the streets, as at Bedford Park. The third estate, at Norbury, was started in the same way, but its western half, which was laid out in 1909, and the contemporary Old Oak estate took on a new pattern. Instead of a grid of streets, across and along, lined by houses, the LCC introduced closes set back from the streets and, at Old Oak, the meandering routes that were to become the hallmark of later council suburbs. The short rows of houses followed their own lines, sometimes coming forward to meet the streets, at others standing back behind greens.

The layouts took full advantage of the latest ideas in planning that were just then being exemplified by Hampstead Garden Suburb. The Suburb was the brain-child of Dame Henrietta Barnett. Her twenty years of experience in working among the poor in Whitechapel led to disgust at the class segregation, ignorance and unregulated urban development of the East End. There was to be no place for that in her ideal suburb, which she founded in 1906. Its design was prompted by her belief in the uplifting nature of art and beauty. Moreover, it would provide homes for rich and poor alike, and there would be a social centre with churches and an institute offering the spiritual and moral benefits of religion and education.

The planners of Hampstead Garden Suburb were Barry Parker and his brother-in-law and partner, Raymond Unwin. They were fresh from their work at Letchworth, the first garden city. Letchworth and the whole garden city movement had been founded by Ebenezer Howard

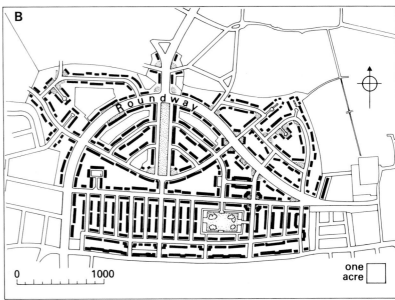

A: The layout of the Old Oak estate. B: The layout of the White Hart Lane estate.
The parts below and to the left of the railway at Old Oak and laid out as a grid across the bottom of White Hart Lane were built before the First World War, the remaining parts following it.

as an attempt at providing an ideal environment for all classes, complete with factories as well as houses. In Howard's words, 'Town and country must be married and out of this joyous union will spring a new hope, a new life and a new civilization.'

In the smaller orbit of the 240 acres devoted to Hampstead Garden Suburb, Parker and Unwin were more successful aesthetically, establishing a pattern of attractive houses round closes, and streets that were neither all straight nor all winding. Always they were laid out so as to exploit the contours of the land, and they joined each other to allow interestingly composed views of the houses and the old trees that were retained on the site.

There was an economic as well as an aesthetic advantage in this arrangement. Where land was cheap, the cost of road construction reached significant proportions. Closes with houses radiating round them, or groups of houses clustered into loose open squares set back from the roadway allowed far more houses to be built for any length of road than a standard terrace would allow. Artistry and economy could come together here, though the design was more difficult.

The new plan allowed for 'open spaces, forming quadrangles, opening one into the other, with wide streets at intervals', as Unwin said in *Cottage Plans and Common Sense*. 'Each square could have some individuality of treatment,' and, all in all, architecture for the poor as well as the rich could be humanised. The Suburb was immediately recognised as a great success for its planning and architecture, and was widely influential. Sadly, though, it never became what Henrietta Barnett wanted. Intellectuals, socialists, the artistic and people of wider sensibility all made their homes here, but the rents of the smallest cottages and the fare of only 2d by Underground railway to central London were not enough of an inducement to bring in a significant number of poorer working-class people. Middle class in conception and in everything else the Suburb has always been. The Central Square, too, never became a true social centre. It lacks shops, pubs, cafés and all the things people want (though there are tennis courts). As Professor Pevsner drily remarked in *The Buildings of England*, 'Institute education and divine worship have not proved to be as much of a permanent and non-intermittent attraction as the social reformers behind the Suburb had hoped for.'

The LCC Housing Branch could not afford such amenities on their smaller and cheaper suburban estates. The Old Oak estate covers only 55 acres and others were smaller still, but even the 226 acres of the White Hart Lane estate were not at first given a cultural, recreational or commercial centre. There was soon a park and then some shops, but although the tenants here continually asked for some kind of communal building and were promised one in 1911, nothing was done until 1948. Even the railway station was ten minutes' walk away. The Old Oak estate was luckier. It had the advantage of its own railway station and cheap fares to London. Five shops were built flanking Erconwald Street at the entrance to the estate, and more were to come later. Further, it followed Hampstead Garden Suburb in its planning, because the picturesque layout that Unwin had persuaded the government to accept as a special case for the benefit of his suburb was now incorporated into the new, general Housing and Town Planning Act of 1909. Picturesque principles were immediately applied to the later part of the Norbury estate and to the Old Oak estate and all that followed.

The purpose of the Act, and indeed of the design of these estates as well, was, in the words of its promoter John Burns when he explained his Bill to Parliament, 'to provide a domestic condition for the people in which their physical health, their morals, their character and their

Chimneys and gables, bricks and tiles. The vernacular image of the White Hart Lane estate.

whole social condition can be improved'. Physical beauty would play as important a role as ordinary physical amenities to improve 'the character of a great people'. In short, Burns looked forward to 'the home healthy, the house beautiful'.

The first of the Old Oak houses were designed between 1909 and 1911, many of them under Archibald Soutar's supervision. He had had experience of designing garden suburbs and model villages in partnership with his better-known brother, J C S Soutar, who was to succeed Unwin at Hampstead Garden Suburb. The Suburb's houses gave Archibald Soutar much of his inspiration for Old Oak. No doubt like hordes of other architects he had visited the Suburb and knew it well, and could also draw on the fairy-tale vision presented by the illustrations in *Town Planning and Modern Architecture at the Hampstead Garden Suburb*, which had made a timely appearance in 1909. In this way the art and beauty that Henrietta Barnett offered to the poor in her own suburb, but which they were never able to afford, were taken by Soutar and the other LCC Housing Branch architects and given to the poor who were meant to live on the Old Oak estate and its successors.

Despite the small sizes of the individual houses, the LCC's Housing Branch architects spared no pains with the detailing, such as the brickwork of the pathway and the linking wall and doorway between two blocks of houses in Risley Avenue, White Hart Lane.

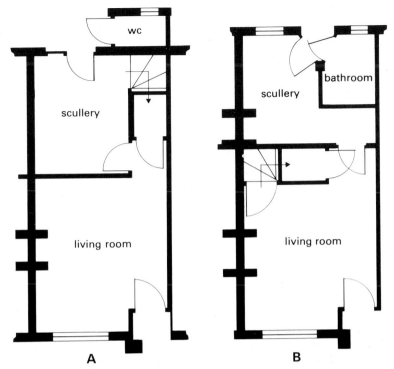

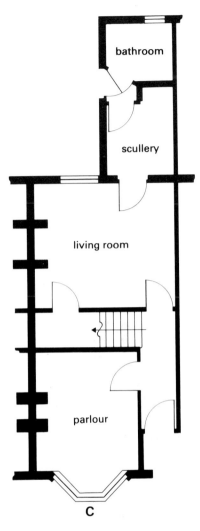

Varieties of house plans on the White Hart Lane estate. A: A four-roomed house with external water-closet. B: A larger four-roomed house with a combined bathroom and water-closet. C: A parlour house with scullery and bathroom in a small rear extension.

Unfortunately the LCC did not entirely succeed in this aim. The size of the houses on their estates was pared down to a minimum in order to keep costs and therefore rents as low as possible. It was an awkward decision. The houses were very small indeed, but their costs were not, and nor were the rents, which were low enough to attract working-class people, but not the poorest of them. Most of the houses had only three or four rooms, so they were not much help to large families who were already living in overcrowded accommodation.

So although the LCC adopted much of the planning and style of the Hampstead Garden Suburb, it could not afford its generous spaciousness where, overall, only eight houses were built to the acre. By comparison, when at last Preston's by-laws enforced wide streets and back lanes, speculative builders there could still raise forty houses to the acre. In their first large cottage estates the LCC had reduced that number to about thirty, and now at Old Oak this was further reduced to twenty-five. That was just low enough to allow the green and leafy aspect of the Hampstead houses to be repeated. Every house indeed had a tiny front garden and more space in a private back garden for healthy recreation and hanging washing, but the individual houses could never have the same breadth as the Hampstead houses nor the access to daylight that went with it. This lack of breadth meant that many front doors at Old Oak were grouped together in pairs under common porches, an endearing way of simplifying the external appearance, unifying the design and hiding the small size of the individual cottages.

Because the houses had to be small and cheap, they had to continue the tradition of the long and narrow plan of speculative terrace houses, though the back extensions of the tunnel-backs were largely avoided. Much odium attached to these extensions, especially in closely packed terraces, because they made the backs notoriously dark and crowded.

Half of the White Hart Lane estate houses had no bathrooms, so the only recourse was to a tin bath, sometimes hung on the back wall, as photographed here in 1985. A programme of enlarging these houses and providing bathrooms is now being undertaken by the London Borough of Haringey.

The small open lobby which divided the scullery from the bathroom for the sake of hygiene.

The Housing Branch architects tackled this by contriving to fit wash-houses, water-closets, coal stores and sometimes bathrooms into the back part of their houses with either no projection or only small ones.

'The cottages look almost as well at the back as they do at the front,' Louis Ambler of the Architectural Association had written after a visit to the Totterdown Fields estate in 1903, 'and the sun and air have full play all round. . . . All the rooms are well lighted and cheerful, and the outlook from each is pleasant.'

The bulk of the houses here and later at White Hart Lane, Norbury and Old Oak had two storeys containing three, four or five main rooms and a small scullery. The smallest houses were very tiny indeed, hardly 12 feet wide and 24 feet deep. The rooms followed the two-up, two-down arrangement so common in Preston, but on an even smaller scale. A pair of bedrooms lay over a front living room and a rear scullery. The living room might only be 12 feet by 13 feet. It had to act as the kitchen, and was given a cooking range for the purpose. The scullery, which might be only 8 feet by 9 feet, was used as a wash-house and store. Coal for the fires was dumped in a cupboard under the stairs. At least these three-roomed houses all had a water-closet, some in a little projection at the rear and entered from outside, while in others it was within the main walls of the house and reached by an open lobby between it and the scullery. Yet again others had both a water-closet and a bath squeezed into this space. Houses without baths had to make do with a tub that was hung on the scullery wall when not in use. For all other washing the tenants had to use the scullery sink, as there was no hand basin.

The four-roomed houses usually provided both a living room and a more formal parlour, and fitted an even smaller scullery, a water-closet and perhaps a bath into a small rear projection. Sometimes the parlour served as a third bedroom. The five-roomed houses were in a minority before the First World War, amounting to only about a tenth of all the houses. They stretched as far as a third bedroom as well as a living room and a parlour; and they sometimes had a bathroom upstairs, if not downstairs, and a separate water-closet.

This division of so small an overall floor area into so many rooms was not entirely of the architects' choosing. In 1902 Unwin had tried to reform the plan of the speculators' two-up, two-down house with its added tunnel-back, and he published his proposals in *Cottage Plans and Common Sense*. He tucked the scullery, water-closet and store cupboards of the rear extension into the main part of his proposed houses. At the same time he knocked together the parlour and living room into one larger and, he believed, more useful, lighter room. Perhaps his thoughts were turning romantically to the all-purpose medieval hall, but his explanation was clear enough. 'However desirable a parlour may be, it cannot be said to be necessary to health or family life,' he wrote; 'it is worse than folly to take space from that living-room, where it will be used every day and every hour, to form a parlour, where it will be used only once or twice a week.'

Unwin was possibly right about the needs of health but quite wrong about the needs of family life. People wanted a separate parlour. Nevertheless, he and Barry Parker designed houses with enlarged living rooms rather than separate living rooms and parlours, and built them on the

The White Hart Lane estate: a group of houses set back from the street around a small court facing Risley Avenue.

Working drawings for cottages built during the first phase of the White Hart Lane Estate, on Risley Avenue and Cheshunte Road.

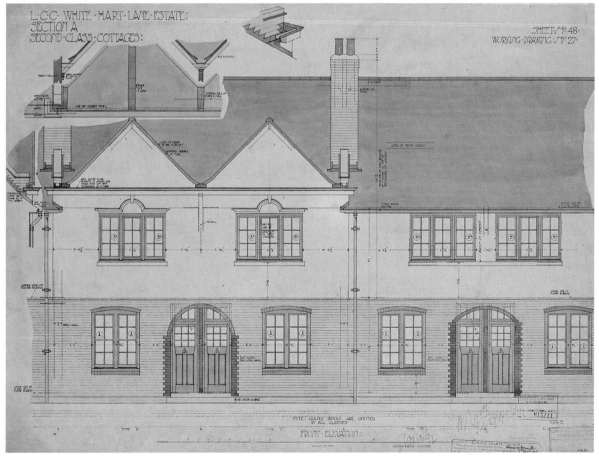

How Hampstead Garden Suburb influenced the design of the LCC cottage estates.
Right: One of the blocks designed by Archibald Soutar at the corner of Du Cane Road and Fitzneal Street, Old Oak LCC Estate.
Below: His model, a corner house in Meadway, Hampstead Garden Suburb. The most significant difference is that the LCC block contains four separate dwellings, while the Meadway house is a single dwelling.

Rowntree estate at New Earswick near York. They should have been very successful, but were criticised for ignoring what working people wanted. The reformers in all their idealistic, socialist zeal wanted to improve people's health and to strengthen family life through the architectural agencies of beauty, sweetness and light. What they failed to realise was that families wanted to have a parlour or 'best room' both to accommodate their most treasured possessions and for formal occasions. It was closer to people's hearts. This need was a warning that rationalist, progressive architects should have heeded: a house can never be simply a machine for living in. It has to be a home.

The living room of a non-parlour house on the White Hart Lane estate, reconstructed for the BBC series House and Home, *with furnishings of the period.*

The LCC's Housing Branch architects did recognise the importance of the parlour, and all but their smallest houses had two downstairs rooms rather than one larger room. The trouble was that the front room, the parlour, could be very small indeed, 10-foot square or less, and could hardly contain both furniture and family, let alone a few formal guests. Sometimes the larger parlours were entered directly from the front door so that they lacked the privacy essential to a formal room.

Unquestionably the greatest amenity provided in these houses was sanitation. All the houses had a water-closet, usually next to the scullery and divided from it for health reasons by an open lobby. Water-closets were now common enough in speculative housing, but not in the older houses generally occupied by the working classes. Newer still were

The parlour, today, in one of the larger houses on the White Hart Lane estate. It is, even so, less than 10 feet square.

Tower Gardens on the White Hart Lane estate, in use above in 1914, and as conceived as a garden, right (c. 1910).

Living a sober, modest, healthy life on the White Hart Lane estate.

bathrooms. About half the houses had these, though usually they combined the bath with the water-closet. Cleanliness and, with it, greater privacy were fresh amenities, previously the preserve of the middle classes, to add to basic sanitary improvements. In the houses without baths, however, there was still no other recourse but to set a tub before the fire in the old way, or to use the scullery sink. The houses were expensive to build, and when structurally complete they had to make their way with little further expenditure on alterations. Penny-pinching ruled, and some houses still have no baths to this day.

On the brighter side, though, these houses were definitely more practical as well as more sanitary than their Victorian predecessors in all but size. Gas provided instant lighting, and electricity was eventually to come. Some houses on the White Hart Lane estate first had electric light in the 1920s, but conversion of the older houses to electricity was completed only in the 1940s. Gas provided instant heating too, not yet for the whole house, but certainly for a copper in the scullery in which to wash clothes, and for a small stove for cooking food. Gas stoves were small enough to go in the scullery and that saved space, but this was a mixed blessing because these rooms were so confined. The living room could then cease to be a kitchen, and its fire had a new use if it was fitted with a back boiler to provide hot running water for a sink and bath.

The LCC's cottage estates were in their larger way intended to be shining beacons of progressive architecture, which was supposed to encourage the occupants to live sober, modest, healthy lives. The Council's agents who managed the estates believed that this would be more readily achieved if prospective tenants were vetted to ensure their respectability before they were accepted and their tenancy agreements required them to maintain it. So neatness, tidiness and cleanliness became the object of numerous conditions of the tenancies, and there were regular inspections to check that the tenants kept up these standards. The result was that the theories behind the progressive architecture and planning of the estates were not at first tested by trying them out

on people who were still thought of as the less deserving of the poor. Somewhere the good intentions were lost. Rather than the architecture of these estates prompting goodness in people, only good people were allowed to taste the architecture.

Tenants had to be more than good. They had to be solvent. Rent was payable weekly, in advance, and there was an initial charge of a few shillings' key money. If you fell a week into arrears you were served notice to quit.

The smallest of the three-roomed houses built before the Great War on the White Hart Lane estate cost £150 to build, and the average cost of the houses there was £281. They were not cheap, given their small size. Though eventually subsidised, rents were consequently fairly high, and the LCC found it hard to let houses at first. Even when the lowest rent was only 6s 6d per week, and the average 9s 6d, the poorest people could not afford to live here.

Some of the paired doorways set within single porches on the White Hart Lane and Old Oak estates.

In the first instance only a few people came from slum clearance areas, and many were not even from overcrowded parts of inner London. They already lived locally and were attracted by all the new amenities.

A majority of tenants did at least belong to the working classes, but generally they were skilled rather than manual workers. One or two are even said to have had occupations such as managing banks and teaching the pianoforte that are not normal ways of making a living for the working class at all. So despite the original intention, the estates were not specifically used to house people made homeless by slum clearances until the 1930s, nor to house people so destitute that they could afford nothing else. The estate managers saw to this, although it was not because they wilfully disregarded policy. It was simply that they had to charge certain rents and were responsible for collecting them. So they chose tenants on the basis of those who could pay, and insisted that they did so. The failure was actually political; the original intention was lost before it could be executed. It was not exactly a policy of 'unto them that hath shall it be given', but in practice it turned into one of 'unto them that hath not shall it not be given'.

Though their intentions were different, as was shown by the design of their estates, the LCC was acting in a way not unlike that of speculative builders. It began with its sights firmly set on providing for the poor and built accordingly, but when it came to letting its cottages it was as determined to safeguard its rents as any other landlord.

The Old Oak estate was the architectural climax of the LCC's suburban developments. Only half was complete before the outbreak of the Great War halted building by local councils. When work resumed afterwards, the LCC continued to exploit the style it had established between 1905 and 1914, though its houses were now generally rather larger. Strangely, it was the war itself that prompted the building of a new cottage estate which pushed this picturesque style to its furthest limits. The opening of the Western Front soon caused a desperate shortage of munitions. In order to meet the demand for shells, the workforce at Woolwich Arsenal was doubled before the end of 1914, and continued to expand. The government had to find accommodation for the workers immediately and acted with amazing speed. By the end of 1915 the Office of Works, under its new architect Frank Baines, had responded by completing the 1000 houses and 200 flats of the Well Hall estate nearby at Eltham. Instead of regiments of barrack-like buildings that might have stood as a symbol of the times, it built pretty groups of cottages clustering around a wonderful maze of streets winding along the flank of Shooters Hill. The estate more than fulfilled all the most picturesque principles of garden suburb planning. The houses were designed with intricately varied forms, using projecting bays, jetties, gables and dormers. They were built in a seemingly endless variety of materials, with combinations of timber-framing, tile-hanging, slate-hanging, weather-boarding, colour-washed rendering, pebble-dash, brick and stone. The immediate reason was to make use of whatever materials might become available during a period of acute wartime shortage, but the underlying intention was to demonstrate to the fullest the qualities of a progressive domestic style whose variety and rural character were believed to have a civilising effect on the inhabitants. Yet here lived the arsenal workers who produced the means of slaughtering regiments and regiments of massed soldiers. It was a strange meeting.

There are again telling contrasts in both appearance and cost between the government's Well Hall estate and the adjacent speculative estates. To the east is Eltham Park, which had been built in the pre-war years by the Liberal MP Archibald Cameron Corbett. Corbett laid out his estate on an old-fashioned grid plan, and built terrace upon terrace of similar houses. His aim was to provide for a range of people, from the moderately poor to the moderately well-to-do, on an estate that he planned specifically with health in mind. All the hygienic benefits of hot and cold running water, bathrooms, water-closets, main drainage and front and back gardens were combined with churches and a prohibition on pubs so that the evils of alcohol should not upset the morals of the inhabitants. There was no attempt to influence them through the style of the houses, however, which was old-fashioned and run-of-the-mill. Corbett sold them at cost, £248 for a three-bedroomed house, rising to £488 for six bedrooms. He took his profit from the annual ground rent, which was about £5 to £10, depending on the size of the plot.

The cheapest houses, with a frontage of 24 feet and three bedrooms as well as parlour, living room and a good-sized scullery–kitchen, compare favourably for their amenities with the houses, for example, on the Old Oak estate where a marginally lower building cost of £150–240 paid for a house with a very narrow frontage, only three rooms and a poky little scullery. The LCC's chief architect called his houses 'brick boxes with very little else', and people grumbled at their high cost, even though it was little enough compared with the houses on the Well Hall estate.

A comparison between the government's Well Hall estate, or, for that matter, any of the LCC's estates, and the estates of men like Corbett leads to much the same conclusion. The picturesque qualities of the Well Hall houses made for complications in their construction and so pushed up the cost. By sticking to a few simple designs, speculators like Corbett could build far more cheaply. Unwin himself realised that cottage design would have to be simplified for financial reasons, and at a second estate for munitions workers at Gretna in Scotland he and the resident architect, Courtnay Crickmer, designed comparatively plain brick boxes with overall hipped roofs only broken where the chimney-stacks rose through them. All the artifice of Well Hall was avoided, and replaced by well-proportioned details harking back to the elegance of the Georgian terrace.

Finally, by 1916 the most up-to-date estate planners regarded William Morris's vision of a handmade Britain not just as an expensive luxury (and perhaps ineffective in improving the character of the inhabitants), but also as a sham. The increasing cost of building caused by the war made simplicity imperative, and this could be justified on social grounds as well. 'The standard cottage will depend for any attraction that it may possess, not upon the toolmarks of the workman, nor upon its peculiarity or idiosyncracy, nor in a word upon its individuality', wrote the planner and architect Stanley Adshead in 1916, 'but upon more general characteristics such as suitability to purpose and excellence of design.'

This sounds remarkably like the principle of functionalism with its insistent disregard for style, yet Adshead's own scheme, designed in partnership with Stanley Ramsey in 1913 for the Duchy of Cornwall estate in Kennington in London, was not only laid out formally with terraces of straight streets and squares, but was dressed in a charming Regency style as well. By the end of the war the simplicity of this Georgian style was being widely adopted, though in far plainer forms, and it soon came to dominate the LCC's later cottage estates, such as Becontree in East London, and those of other housing authorities. Many of their estates came to look exceedingly plain, and, because of the great size of many of them, very tedious as well.

During the war there had been a great debate on what kind of housing should be built afterwards. When conscription was introduced in 1916, the shockingly poor health of the conscripts was exposed to public scrutiny in the clearest light. By the last year of the war four out of every ten of them were being graded C3 and unfit for any military service, let alone the trenches. Poor housing was widely blamed, and the government realised that it would have to do more after the war to eradicate it. Many soldiers had left the slums for France never to return; those who survived should have something better to come home to.

There had to be greater social justice. Two immediate results of the awareness of this need were universal adult male suffrage with, for the first time, votes for women on a limited basis, and the founding of the Ministry of Reconstruction. Under Christopher Addison's direction it set up committees to survey practically every aspect of British life. It was a clear demonstration of how extensively the state accepted that it had obligations to its citizens. Some of this was little more than window-dressing, but there were achievements and among these were the recommendations of the Women's Housing Sub-committee. Despite women's immense contribution to wartime industry, this sub-committee accepted that a woman's chief task was to make a home. 'The working woman with a home of her own will be a voter,' said one of its reports. 'Let her first effort of citizenship be to improve this home.' A survey of new housing estates and a questionnaire circulated among working women formed the basis of two published reports by the committee and numerous recommendations were made for improving workers' housing. Further reports that criticised architects' plans for housing were not published on the flimsy grounds that this would mean reprinting the plans.

The Women's Sub-committee nevertheless did influence the work of the Local Government Board's Tudor Walters Committee, and its own report, written by Raymond Unwin in 1918, made recommendations for the future provision of workers' housing. It set standards for all the houses built between the wars, and was the basis for newer standards until long afterwards:

THE WORKING WOMAN'S HOUSE

BY
A.D. SANDERSON FURNISS
& MARION PHILLIPS

ILLUSTRATED

LONDON
THE SWARTHMORE PRESS LTD.
72 Oxford Street W.1.   PRICE 1s 6d NET

The cover of the Women's Housing Sub-committee report. Although the illustration disregards architectural style as such, it clearly favours the ideals of the garden suburb.

> We regard it as essential that each house should contain as a minimum three rooms on the ground floor (living-room, parlour and scullery) and three bedrooms above – two of these being capable of containing two beds. A larder and a bathroom are essential.

The report specified minimum sizes of rooms and suggested that the smallest house should have at least 855 square feet of floor space, where the LCC's smallest had had less than 600 square feet. The recommended minimum for a six-roomed house was 1 055 square feet where the LCC's had been about 950 square feet. Much of this confirmed the wishes of the Women's Housing Sub-committee, whose own report had also emphasised that the scullery should be large enough to function as the working centre of the house, and that there should be improved methods of heating and better hot-water systems to reduce unnecessary drudgery.

Immediately after the Great War there was a burst of house building by local councils, thanks to the unlimited subsidies offered by Addison's Ministry of Reconstruction. But within two years runaway costs and alarming inflation had brought the system into disrepute and Addison was made a scapegoat. Council house building was curtailed, and the houses built thereafter seldom fulfilled the recommendations of the Tudor Walters Report. The Women's Housing Sub-committee felt betrayed.

Eventually, however, as building costs fell during the next decade, private industry took the initiative and was able to do what Corbett had already demonstrated before the war by building larger houses than the councils had built and at a lower cost. It could compete successfully in other significant ways too, for instance by offering houses for sale with cheap mortgage facilities. Nevertheless, the councils with the LCC at their head had established themselves as local housing authorities and were to build a million dwellings before the outbreak of the Second World War. Housing and politics now had a firm grasp of each other. Increasingly, the poor could look to public housing as a means of obtaining a home at a rent that they could afford.

After the First World War, soaring costs of house building made it necessary to simplify and standardise designs. Here in Henningham Road on the White Hart Lane estate, the post-war houses used the popular neo-Georgian style which, among other things, substituted plain hipped roofs for the varied gables of the earlier houses.

CHAPTER SEVEN
Semi-detached Suburbia

When the Second World War started in 1939 there were four million new houses in Great Britain. All were less than twenty years old, most less than ten. Two-thirds had been built by speculative builders for sale to newly affluent people who were laying the foundations of our present consumer society. Their wealth was evident in the wonderful variety of household goods in the shops. Their leisure and house-ownership between them made the home a centre of consumption, not just of necessities like food, clothing and furniture, but of all kinds of novelties that helped to impress the owner's individuality on it.

The ultimate possession to which any household aspired was a motor car. It gave people a new freedom to leave their homes whenever they wished. It let them visit their friends, go to the sea for holidays and picnic in the countryside that their own homes had helped to erode. Two million cars, mainly owned by the middle classes, now had the run of the freshly laid concrete of miles of new arterial roads.

Cars were a recent innovation, and were for the first time being built cheaply in great numbers. Roads had less that was new about them, but their construction was now in the hands of a modernised industry employing mechanical diggers and rollers and factory-made cement delivered by motor lorry. A more significant development was that, unlike the railways of the nineteenth century, the roads were built under the auspices of the state and with state capital. Since the start of the Great War the state had become widely involved in people's affairs with the aim of promoting their welfare. In fact, a secondary purpose behind the road-building programme was to provide work for labourers at a time of mass unemployment. But despite the great number

The new fast Rochester by-pass road in the 1930s on a day when it was not so fast. It is already lined on one side with new houses.

of council houses built immediately after the Great War, housing had not also become largely a state undertaking.

What was astonishing about the houses was their very newness. The four million built in the twenty years of peace from 1919 to 1939 amounted to between a third and a half of the total housing stock in the country. Never had so many houses been built so quickly.

- The new houses were everywhere, especially on the outskirts of Midland and southern towns. This was because the centre of production of the nation's wealth was moving southwards to where the new light industries were located, and away from the old northern sources of wealth such as mining, steel-making, ship-building and textiles. Any of the proud new owners taking their car for a spin along one of the new arterial roads leading out of London would see the new, low, clean factories and thousands of new houses around them. Whether Eastern Avenue or Western Avenue, Edgware Way or the Kingston by-pass, the Great West Road or Rochester Way, they would speed past mile after mile of these brand-new houses before ever reaching the open country. Indeed, they would see the countryside being consumed by the streets of rising houses, all as alike as the cars on the roads.

Most of these houses were semi-detached, and had a living room, dining room and kitchen downstairs, and three bedrooms above. Each one was as like its neighbours and all the semi-detached houses in the country as an Austin was like a Ford or Hillman or Morris. Just as cars (if people could afford them) were usually bought on hire purchase rather than with cash, so a house was usually obtained on a mortgage.

This was again new. The inflation that so quickly followed the Great War soon enforced government economies, cut short Addison's open-ended subsidies and reduced the number of houses that the state could afford to build. The fixed subsidies paid per house that Neville Chamberlain introduced in 1923 did little to encourage state housing, but were a greater incentive to builders to provide houses for sale. Meanwhile, because the rent controls introduced during the war remained in force, the construction of houses to rent out lost its attraction. Encouraged by tax concessions, capital went instead to building societies which provided the mortgages that enabled people to buy their own homes. Before the Great War less than a tenth of all houses in Great Britain were owner-occupied. By 1939 this proportion had increased threefold to nearly 30 per cent. One way or another capital was increasingly organised to encourage consumption, and at the heart of this lay the home.

These changes are clearly evident round the old village of Bexley. If you drove down into Kent, perhaps for a day by the sea at Herne Bay or Margate, you would not have bothered with the old, constricted Roman road over Shooters Hill to Dartford. Instead, you would have taken the fast by-pass called Rochester Way. If you went in 1924, the year the road was completed, you would have crossed heathland that was still open and allowed occasional views of Bexley and lonely country houses such as Blendon Hall. The scrubby nature of the land and the poverty of the soil accentuated the depressed state of the farms on each side of the road, but the underlying sand and gravel gave the area great potential for building as it was well drained and so provided good foundations. In 1934, ten years later, this was all too clear, and by 1939 the view had been utterly transformed. For 3 miles you would now pass through the Urban District of Bexley, and semi-detached houses stretched to the horizon left and right. The farms had gone, and so had Blendon Hall. All you could see of the old village of Bexley was a distant church spire. The new landmark at the turning off the main road for the village was the Black Prince road-house. Designed to serve new motorists and the new population of suburbanites, it was really no more than a giant pub done up like a hotel and given the gentility of waitress service rather than the rough scrum of crowded bars. Nevertheless, it needed a bit of character so it was decked out with mock half-timbering and tall Tudoresque chimneys.

Many of the semi-detached houses were decorated with a bit of mock timbering too, but there were alternatives in the form of cement rendering, exposed brickwork, tile-hanging, and pebble-dash. In fact, not all the houses were semi-detached; a glance showed that some of them, otherwise identical, were strung out into terraces of four, six or even eight houses. Conversely, here and there one was sliced off from its partner and stood completely detached like a lone Siamese twin. Others seemed to be sliced off horizontally and were without a second storey: they were bungalows. Yet others had outside staircases to the upper storey and were flats.

Despite all these differences – and the list is endless – the overall impression we have today is of a general uniformity. But that is not the impression an engaged couple got when they set out to buy one of these houses so that they could marry and set up home. Each weekend they could search through pages of advertisements in the newspapers. Every locality claimed to be different. Every estate had its particular features. Every house was presented as uniquely tailored especially for them. On Saturdays, the *Evening News* ran 'The Homeseekers' Guide', where builders extolled the competing virtues of their houses. Morrells invited you to 'open your window to the tonic air of Kent's healthiest estates' where they offered sixty-one different types of house, and

Leo Meyers' Hurst Road estate at Bexley with the roads laid out and stacks of bricks already delivered. At the bottom right is one of the farms, looking out across its fields for the last time before they are obliterated by the building works.

emphasised that 'You'll **remember Chelsfield** as the finest estate you have ever seen'. Meanwhile, Wates ('the quality builders') offered a choice of '15 lovely estates' spread across the south of London from Abbey Wood to Worcester Park, and invited home seekers to send for a free art book. Here they would discover just how differently styled all these essentially similar houses were, what wonderful modern amenities they offered and how cheap and easy they were to buy.

In the 1920s Edward and Arthur Wates were laying the foundations of their firm in Streatham by taking advantage of Chamberlain's government subsidies, then running at £120 per house. These encouraged small house builders, and buyers too because they kept prices down. Wates were then selling their houses for £650 freehold or £55 cash down and weekly repayments of 25s 6d. If you had saved some capital and had a decent income you might agree with their advertisements that this was 'much better than rent'. By 1935 the message was all persuasive. The cost of building had fallen, and house prices generally ranged from £400 to £1 500. Moreover, the amount of capital available to building societies for mortgages had risen so far that down-payments were slashed to around £5, which could be borrowed from the builders, and the repayments started at 8s 10d. Some builders would even guarantee these payments, so anxious were they to sell. You would be lucky to rent a comparable house so cheaply. At these prices Wates' houses offered electricity, gas, hot and cold running water, and, except in the cheapest ones, space for a garage. The houses were fully guaranteed, and, as a final reassurance, the roads and pavements of even the newest estate were already laid. To entice people into this new world of house-ownership, display offices welcomed them daily until 7 pm at Lewisham and Peckham, the run-down inner suburbs they hoped to escape from, as well as at Streatham, where the firm had started, and in the City where perhaps they worked.

The potential owners might be bank clerks or employees in commercial enterprises earning £4 or £5 a week and with prospects of promotion. They might be starting out in one of the new industries at £3 a week, still 5s above the average national wage. At all events, they would be in the lucky position of having gained from the Industrial Revolution and a century of the heavy industry that had built up so much wealth that there were immense surpluses of capital looking for new fields of employment.

There was capital for motor cars, and a wide range of light industries such as electrical engineering that manufactured goods for the home. There was capital too for services like banking and insurance that promoted the financing of the building boom, and for commerce and the distributive trades that kept the new society going. Most significantly, there was capital from the immense number of investors who were frightened of putting their money into old industries at a time of depression and believed that nowhere was as safe as houses. They swelled the funds in building societies tenfold between the wars to reach £700 million by 1939, and it all went out in cheap mortgages.

New industries, services and commerce between them produced goods tailored both to meet and encourage the new demand for them.

This needed a new labour force of clerks and technicians, foremen and salesmen, managers and specialists, not to mention skilled workers.

Anyone who could benefit from the education that had been made compulsory since the Education Act of 1870, or who had the eye to see the new opportunities, had the chance of gaining from the new prosperity. Labourers, on the other hand, who relied on muscle alone and toiled in the heavy industry that had fed the Industrial Revolution in the nineteenth century, provided work that was badly paid, if it was wanted at all. They remained poor.

The new affluence had swollen the middle class from a fifth of the population in 1911 to not far short of a third by the Second World War. Moreover, there were also people at the upper end of the working class who, though not affluent, were at least able to afford far more than the bare necessities of life. Meanwhile, the growth of the population itself had slackened, although people were marrying earlier than ever and the number of family units consequently rose. The difference was that a couple now tended to have two or three children, not five or six, and they all generally survived infancy.

There were two consequences of these social changes for housing. First, these new families increased the demand for houses, and many people now had the money to buy them. Second, because wealth had raised people's expectations, they wanted their houses to be big enough to accommodate all the newly available amenities, to provide more privacy, and to furnish with the increased number of household goods that they could now afford.

The smaller size of families freed women from endless child-bearing and nursing, and potentially gave them greater opportunity for employment. This though did not generally happen in the 1920s and 1930s. Before marriage women were now often in paid work. Poorer women still worked in domestic service if not in factories and mills. Educated, middle-class women filled many clerical and administrative posts or became teachers. But social custom and the difficult economic conditions of the Depression conspired to ensure that on marriage women left their work and returned to the houses where they were commonly supposed to belong. However good a woman was at her job, her life was widely held to culminate in marriage, and she was judged a failure if she was unable to catch a husband.

As they always had been, the home and marriage were vital to each other. The suburban house formalised the roles within marriage more strongly than ever. It was the husband's job to provide the income to run it, and the housewife's job to provide the labour and management to keep it going. During the week from 7.30 to 8 am when the trains and buses took the men off to their city offices and new factories to 6 or 6.30 pm when they brought them back again, the home was the preserve of the women alone. It was not exactly purdah, but the only men you saw during the day in suburban estates like those around Bexley were on their delivery rounds. It was opportunity rather than unusual charm that gave milkmen and window cleaners their notorious reputations.

A woman's work was mapped out. From Monday's washing to Friday's weekend shopping at the often distant shops, a routine of household chores and care of the children kept housewives busy. The home beautiful – that is to say, the whole house spotless and shining – was, and still is, the ideal of every advertisement for household products, and it was widely accepted by the new housewives and expected by

Women's magazines promoted the idea of the modern, capable, efficient housewife, here applying herself to DIY in an advertisement from Modern Home *in 1930. Notice how her 'husband' is quoted as encouraging this role.*

their husbands. The idea of the modern, capable, efficient housewife was invented then as a centre of consumption. As she was likely to be newly married, she would be particularly keen to show her husband that she was as competent about the house as she had been in the job she had just left. There were plenty of weekly magazines to offer advice on how to achieve this, and the daily papers had regular woman's pages. These tended to take the place of support from parents, often now left behind with the move out to the suburbs.

The chances were that she would soon have a couple of children and, if things were planned properly, not more than a couple. Then she would be really tied to the house. Motherhood was another sphere in which a woman was expected to shine by putting into practice all the advice in the magazines and mother's guides that, once more, were a substitute for nearby parents.

The husband was also anxious to please. If his prospects turned out to be as good as he hoped, they might possibly be able to afford a charwoman. This would cost 10d to 1s 3d an hour, so if someone came regularly each morning it was quite an extravagance. One or two mornings a week was more usual. If the husband's earnings had reached the £500 to £600 bracket, a couple could just afford a living-in maid, and she would help with the children as well as do domestic chores. Living-in maids were not hard to come by at the Labour Exchange, for many girls came down south from the depressed north of England looking for their fortune. Becoming a living-in maid was a good way for them to start. They got their meals and a roof over their heads and £1 or 25s a week. They did not need much training, and although the work was dull it was not too onerous. Many living-in maids had their sights on better things, and a housewife had to be careful to stipulate that there were to be no 'followers' in the house. If 'unreliable' girls did 'get into trouble' they had to go.

The Second World War and the social and economic changes that followed brought widespread living-in domestic service – a custom that went back to the Middle Ages – to an end. It was secondary education and competing opportunities of employment in the 1940s which finally killed it off after half a century of decline. Housewives who had had domestic servants now had to turn to daily or weekly 'helps' and an increasing range of labour-saving domestic appliances.

Throughout the 1920s and 1930s, these appliances were at least in part sold as status symbols. Competing products were widely advertised in the daily papers and weekly magazines, and the advertisements stressed that the new appliances were a great aid to managing a household on the most modern scientific principles. This was designed to overcome the prejudice of middle-class housewives against doing household chores themselves instead of leaving them to their domestic servants. Housewives might be more willing to do the chores with, say, the help of a Hoover, and it would in any case make the work of a maid or a charwoman more efficient. Only this new appliance or that household product would set the seal of perfection on their housewifely efforts. Such advertising was aimed at women because they managed the household. It was they who decided what to buy, even though they would have to persuade their husbands that here was money well spent, because they were the wage earners.

'Cooking, cleaning, washing, ironing and the manifold tasks of the housewife' all made simple in Miss Magnet's Ideal Home.

It was electricity that made all these goods possible and brought the most dramatic change to the house. The first innovation was electric lighting, which all the new semi-detached suburban houses had, and eventually there was a power point in each room as well, so there could be light anywhere at the flick of a switch. Electric light was not just instant, it was clean and needed no more attention than the occasional replacement of a bulb.

Only two electric labour-saving appliances were widely used then, vacuum cleaners and irons. Vacuum cleaners made cleaning carpets a more effective operation as well as a speedier one. A Hoover cost about £20 just after the Great War, equivalent to as much as four months' mortgage repayments, so you would probably have bought it on hire-purchase, and there was still more to pay for servicing. As demand and production rose though, the price fell by about half to around £10 twenty years later. Even then a Hoover cost as much as a daily help four hours a week for a whole year. Today, the cost of a vacuum would pay for a daily for only six weeks on the same basis. Electric irons were a great boon, especially the later ones that had a regulo to control their temperature so that new artificial fabrics like rayon would not melt when ironed. Irons, again, were not yet particularly cheap and, at between 25s and 35s, cost the same as twenty-five or thirty-five hours' work by a daily help. Today, you could employ a daily for only three or fours hours for the price of a plain iron.

Many housewives had sewing machines, either treadle-operated or occasionally electric. An electric sewing machine cost a lot more than a Hoover, but it offered plenty of savings. With a machine you could make all the curtains for your house at a fraction of the price of specially made curtains from a shop. As for clothes, not only would they be much cheaper if you made them yourself, but if you were skilled they would also fit better and be far more fashionable. Ready-made clothes in the shops were by no means as cheap and up-to-date as they are now. Knitting was also a widespread activity, and both shops and magazines catered for the needlewoman. Once again, a few pennyworth of wool gave you the opportunity to save several shillings on the cost of socks and jumpers and cardigans.

Other labour-saving devices, such as washing machines and dish-washers, were extremely rare before the Second World War, but electric toasters, kettles, cookers and refrigerators were all readily available and provided alternatives to gas appliances. During the 1930s the gas and electricity industries fought each other hard for every customer. Refrigerators came rather slowly into use between the wars, though many builders provided a refrigerator as well as a 'labour-saving' kitchen with fitted cupboards, tiling round a sink and draining-boards, and even a cooker as special inducements to buy their houses. Refrigerators and the arrival of cheap, tinned food made the separate pantry or larder largely redundant, but housewives still expected larders in their new houses, and, even though these could easily take a bite of 10 to 20 square feet out of the kitchen space, builders continued to provide them. Tiled and mirrored bathrooms were another sign of the modern house, and, like fitted kitchens, builders made a special feature of them in their brochures. The all-electric house was the ultimate symbol of modernity, but it was rare and expensive enough to be more of a dream-house than a significant contribution to domestic bliss. However modern the inside, its outer appearance was usually traditional. Houses with all the features of the continental Modern Movement in architecture, such as concrete walls, long bands of metal-framed windows and flat roofs, were only for the avant-garde. Though a few of these features were applied to ordinary brick, semi-detached houses, they were not very popular.

Although electric fires were easily available, they were generally used to supplement older forms of heating. They warmed up quickly, but a coal fire, once it was burning well, eventually gave out far more heat. A fire was the recognised focus of a room, so much so that Magicoal produced a range of electric fires which incorporated simulated glowing coals in their design to make electric heating more acceptable. Gas fires gave out more heat than electricity did, but they could smell, and some people said they gave you headaches and were bad for the complexion because they dried the atmosphere.

A significant advance was central heating. A single solid-fuel boiler provided hot water that circulated round a number of radiators as well as serving a bath and wash-basins. With full built-in central heating you needed an open fire only for show. This combination was rare in semi-detached houses. Stoking the boiler was the hardest and most tyrannical of household chores. Sometimes the men took on the burden, at least of filling the hods of coal. Forget the boiler for an hour or two in the evening, and it might go out. Even a change of wind could increase the draught and cause it to burn out rapidly, leaving you with ash and clinker to clear and all the filth and fuss of laying a new fire.

Electricity brought one immense change in the house – communication. As the vast extent of semi-detached suburbs obliterated the intimate sense of community of old villages like Bexley, the telephone opened up the more abstract community of the whole country to personal conversation, and the wireless brought the country – and, indeed, the world – into your living room. News, sport, entertainment, music, education and children's programmes were all there at the turn of a knob and some careful tuning. By the 1950s television was pushing the process onwards, and these advances are by no means at an end today. The £15 or £20 you paid for a good wireless was a fortune by today's standards, but a bargain compared with a piano, which, as the centre of family entertainment, was soon eclipsed. A gramophone gave you your own choice of music whenever you wanted it. Family talent withered before His Master's Voice.

Indeed, the way in which commercial products from tinned baked beans to Beecham conducting Beethoven came into the home gave a sceptical young poet like John Betjeman the feeling that life had taken on an artificial, lazy quality:

In labour-saving homes, with care
Their wives frizz out peroxide hair
And dry it in synthetic air
    And paint their nails.

(Slough)

It is too easy for outsiders to sneer at the lives women led in their semi-detached homes. Their lives may not have been poetic (though Sir John

The modern kitchen run by electricity, represented by an iron, a kettle and a stove. The message of the photograph is cleanliness rather than the usual bustle surrounding the reality of cooking.

The new modern convenience of a tiled bathroom with hot and cold running water in a New Ideal Homestead house as advertised at £595 freehold.

BEAUTIFUL HOMES IN   COUNTRY SURROUNDINGS

HEALTH THE VITAL FACTOR—   HIGH GROUND FOR HEALTH

GRAVEL SOIL MEANS A DRY   YOU CANNOT WRITE A CHEQUE
HOUSE   FOR HEALTH—

BUT YOU CAN CHOOSE YOUR HOME IN THESE HEALTH-GIVING SURROUNDINGS
NEAR LONDON — YET IN THE COUNTRY

Glorious Park Estate
The Brampton

amid natural woods
open heath

Houses of Charm and Distinction.
Entirely Brick Built on Concrete Foundations.
Estate facing Glorious Woods and open Heath
The very Site hundreds have waited for.
Many Charming Designs—up to date in planning and of excellent appearance.
The talk of Greater London.
Houses of lasting Quality and Value.
"Highest Marks" awarded by Surveyors and Architects for Design, Quality, and Construction.
Garage Site and Private Drive to every House.

NO   NO
ROAD   TERRACES OF
LEGAL OR   HOUSES ON
OTHER CHARGES   THIS ESTATE

LONG GARDENS FRONT AND BACK.
ALL " F. & R." HOUSES ARE OF BEST SELECTED MATERIALS.
HIGH-GRADE JOINERY MADE IN OWN WORKSHOPS
ARTISTRY AND UTILITY COMBINED.   EVERY CONVENIENCE.
DECORATIONS TO CHOICE

THINK OF   AND LIVE ON THIS
YOUR HEALTH !   GLORIOUS HEALTH-
                              GIVING SITE

THE FINAL WORD———"HOMES OF HAPPY DECISION"

Health was always a strong selling point for suburbia. Here, every quality of Bexley's topography from gravel soil to glorious woods underlines the message – that it is an ideal place to bring up your family.

Betjeman came to view suburbia far more rosily after the Second World War), but at least they were not fighting the endless battle against dirt or confined by the continual child-bearing of the previous century. True, suburban women were isolated and their lives were restricted by today's standards, but for many, life in their new houses was bliss. They believed that they had everything they could expect, and far more than their mothers ever dreamed of.

So far as their houses were concerned, people largely had what they wanted. This dismayed the progressive architects and planners, who did not approve of the separate living and dining rooms, and hated both the shoddy architectural values displayed by semi-detached houses and their endless sprawl. The builders, on the other hand, understood exactly what would sell. Some, like Leo Meyer, who founded New Ideal Homesteads and built much of Bexley's suburbs, even went to America to study the most up-to-date methods of salesmanship. This entailed finding out what people wanted, producing it at the lowest possible price and convincing the consumers that their house, just like any other product, was exactly what they wanted. In practice it meant that speculative builders were able to offer women most of what the Women's Housing Sub-committee and the Tudor Walters Report had recommended at the end of the Great War. Architectural artistry and the picturesque planning and landscaping of the estates was of less importance to the occupants than the efficient planning of the houses.

The smallest semi-detached houses had a floor area of about 800 square feet, but 1000–1200 square feet was usual. The main entrance gave access to an entrance hall with a staircase in it. There were no dark corridors, and all the rooms were self-contained and private. The houses usually had four rooms of well over 10 feet square, a living room, a second room used as a dining-room or perhaps a parlour, and two bedrooms. The bedrooms could each take two beds, and there was in addition a third, smaller bedroom for a single bed. This enabled parents, sons and daughters to sleep apart, and exactly conformed with what the Women's Housing Sub-committee had wanted. So too did the privacy downstairs, where a separate kitchen ensured that guests in the living or dining room could remain blissfully unaware of the cooking. Similarly, upstairs a separate bathroom and usually a separate water-closet added to the sense of privacy and propriety already established by the bedrooms. These features were all more or less standard, but a variety of sizes of rooms and of decorative features allowed an increasing choice as you moved up the price range.

The houses were always set back from the road and had small front gardens. These served as a barrier between the public thoroughfare and the privacy of the house, another feature the Women's Housing Sub-committee had recommended. Otherwise, the front gardens were for show. Here a few house-owners arranged a group of garden gnomes and gave the semi-detached house one of its most potent sources of ridicule. Another of these was its name plate, though for every house archly called 'Dunroamin' or 'Bidawee' there were a thousand called 'Hillview' or 'Meadowcroft' (more in hope than truth) and for every one of these there were a thousand labelled 'Twelve' or simply '236'. Names were not essential, but without a number, no milkman or window-cleaner could have coped, let alone the postman.

*Contrasts in advertising.
Left: Leo Meyers' Albany Park estate.
Below: D C Bowyer's Blendon Hall estate. Although some of Bowyer's houses followed standardised patterns, those advertised did not, but Meyers' New Ideal Homesteads were built with little variation by the thousand.*

A pair of Leo Meyers' semi-detached houses on his Hurst Road estate. The one on the right is more or less as built, but the left-hand house has had its porch extended.

Details ancient and modern in Bexley. A sunburst of 'old timbers' contrasting with an Art Deco porch and front door with jazzy glazing and modern movement steel-framed windows.

There was usually a passage round the side of a semi-detached house leading to the back garden. This was also intended to be private. Good fences with trellis and creepers above them kept back gardens from overlooking each other, though you could always peep at your neighbours from a bedroom window.

The advantage of the semi-detached plan was its compromise between the economy of materials in the shared wall of a terrace plan and the easy access to the rear of a house that did not extend to the full width of its plot. This also gave you the opportunity of using the side space for a garage if it was wide enough. The houses were invariably arranged so that one was the mirror-image of the other. The entrances to the two houses of a pair were placed together in the centre in earlier semi-detached houses because this helped to make the pair look like a single house. That pretence was soon abandoned, however, and by the later 1920s the entrances were often put in the further corners of the front, so maintaining as great an illusion of separation as possible. The open flank wall had the advantage of allowing a side entrance to the kitchen for tradesmen, or even a main entrance to the house in some plans, and it also allowed a window to light the staircase, which usually rose against this wall. The living and dining rooms were usually placed at the front and back against the shared party wall, and so the chimney-stacks serving the fireplaces in these rooms were also built against this wall. Being internal, it was a warm wall and some heat from your neighbour's fires could also pass through it, a worthwhile advantage even if you did sometimes hear the noise of your neighbour's wireless coming through it too. In the majority of semi-detached houses the front room had a projecting bay window and the bedroom above followed suit. The backs almost never had bays like this, but the rear room had French doors opening out into the garden.

The semi-detached house had been moderately popular in the nineteenth century as it gave a more rural appearance to a pair of houses than they would otherwise have had as part of a terrace. Status came into it too as they could more easily be mistaken for a single,

The living-room of a semi-detached house as shown in a contemporary catalogue, complete with three vases of flowers and the obligatory three-piece suite.

highly fashionable villa. They did not need as much land as a villa, but they still needed more than a terrace house. In fact, the semi-detached plan became economically possible for cheap houses only because the price of land was not a major consideration. Land was extremely cheap between the wars because of both the continuing depressed state of agriculture and the lack of restrictions on building. As M C Carr has shown in his study of Bexley (*The Development and Character of a Metropolitan Suburb: Bexley, Kent*, 1982), land was little over £200 an acre in the 1920s, and though this price had trebled by 1939 it was still a small proportion of the total building cost.

When Leo Meyer's New Ideal Homesteads company began to build its Hurst Road and Albany Park estates in 1932 on the sites of two farms near Blendon Hall, the average price of a plot of land was £20, whereas the houses that the firm built sold for £395 to £580.

Because they were being sold so cheaply, the houses were closely packed together at about fifteen to the acre, significantly fewer than on some council estates, but nearly double the eight proposed by Bexley Urban District Council. This was part of a widespread but rather ineffective policy in the early 1930s among local authorities to regulate the density of housing. The layout of the streets on these estates followed a very diluted form of what Hampstead Garden Suburb had established and many a council had followed. Picturesque principles concerned the builders less than how to fit a good number of plots on to sites which were often awkward without having recourse to the dreary grid plan. There were seldom the closes set back from the streets favoured elsewhere, because this made access from vehicles difficult, but the streets curved in whatever direction best exploited the shape of the available land rather than its contours. Because this always left numerous odd corners or pieces of back land, culs-de-sac were added to the street pattern to fill them. The cul-de-sac soon became a term of opprobrium closely associated with the dense lay-out of estates of semi-detached houses. New Ideal Homesteads hoped to add several culs-de-sac to their Albany Park estate, but local protests at the density of

A corner of the Hurst Road estate, laid out to follow the curve of a former boundary line rather than to conform with picturesque garden suburb principles.

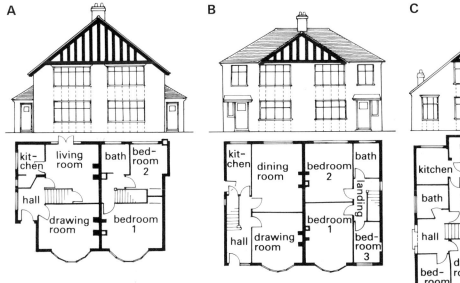

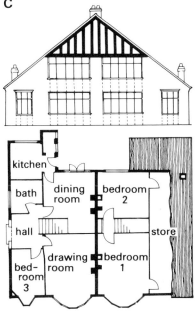

the lay-out caused them to be omitted. This left much wasted land, but even so the overall density was half as high again as was recommended.

New Ideal Homesteads were building to attract customers at the very bottom of the market. It was the low social class of these customers rather than the visual impact of monotonously similar, densely packed houses, that spurred local people to protest about the estate. 'The thing was a disgrace in an area such as old Bexley,' said a local councillor later. Nevertheless, all kinds of people wanted to buy these cheap houses. There were the moderately paid workers employed in the industries along the Thames and clerks who were willing to commute to the City from Albany Park station, which New Ideal Homesteads had persuaded the Southern Railway to open. To have a solid house of their own was a marvel to those new householders.

Some houses were built not as semi-detached dwellings but, for the sake of economy, in terraces of up to eight. Their plans were nevertheless the same. Indeed, in order to keep costs to the minimum everything was standardised and bought in bulk, even from abroad if building materials there were cheaper than at home. New Ideal Homesteads imported bricks from Belgium and door and window frames from Czechoslovakia and landed them at Erith, barely 4 miles away on the Thames. Cement came by road from works only a little further down the Thames, and sand and gravel were abundant locally. With a low-paid workforce on piece rates and encouraged to put in as much overtime as possible, a house could be run up within three weeks. Total output reached a hundred a month, yet despite the speed and despite these quantities, there is no evidence of any jerry-building, either here or on other similar estates generally. In total, New Ideal Homesteads built 1 200 houses on the Hurst Road and Albany Park estates in 1932 and 1933, and a further 2 300 houses a little nearer to London flanking Rochester Way at Falconwood. Here too the firm persuaded the Southern Railway to open a station.

In the 1930s the annual number of houses completed in the country amounted to nearly 350 000. New Ideal Homesteads had 3 000 employees in Bexley and in one record month in 1933 sold nearly 1 000 houses.

Some variations on semi-detached houses, as offered by the Ideal Homesteads in 1935. The ground floors are shown to the left, the upper floors to the right. A and C, with their long, sloping roofs, were often called 'chalet-houses', as distinct from the more usual B, with its central gable projecting in front of the main, hipped roof.
A: House type Q, £575.00 freehold, 14/6 weekly,
B: House type KS, £695.00 freehold, 17/4 weekly,
C: House type A, £725.00 freehold, 18/– weekly.

Building under way. Mass-produced window frames lie ready so that the bricklayers will not be delayed for a moment.

Nevertheless, of the 76 000 builders in the country only just over 1 000 employed more than 100 men, and most employed fewer than ten.

Among the middling builders was another local firm, D C Bowyer and Sons, who had built an estate of bungalows at Bexleyheath. They purchased Blendon Hall and its 88-acre estate, and started building on it in 1929. The original intention was to keep the old house, but in the end it came down to allow the houses fronting Beechway to be built. The same story was being retold all over the country, although restrictions on building imposed as a condition of land sale required a lower density of building and more expensive houses than New Ideal Homesteads had put up. Bowyer had to build the smaller ones with a minimum value of over £700 and £800 at eight to the acre, the larger ones with a minimum value of £1 000 at only six to the acre.

The differences between Bowyer's houses and the nearby New Ideal Homesteads' are clear enough. Not only are Bowyer's larger and more widely spaced, but the winding streets are more attractively laid out and the houses have a greater variety of stylistic treatments. A few even have some of the stylistic tricks of the supposedly style-less architecture of the Modern Movement, such as flat roofs, cement-rendered walls and bands of steel-framed windows.

Unlike those of the New Ideal Homesteads estate, Bowyer's houses sold slowly, and not just because of the unpopularity of the modern style. The houses were cost-wise at the top end of the market for Bexley, and so most people who could afford Bowyer's prices were perhaps put off by the large numbers of cheap New Ideal Homesteads houses nearby and went elsewhere. The lack of rush to buy limited the rate of building, and the last part of the estate was not completed until long after the Second World War. In one way the councillors of old Bexley were wrong and New Ideal Homesteads right: people whose low incomes might cause old Bexley to protest wanted to live here because their workplaces were not far away. Once New Ideal Homesteads had established the cheapest owner-occupier houses and these had become popular, they were self-perpetuating and discouraged anything better that was aimed at people whose greater affluence was more acceptable to local standards. So Bowyer's Blendon Hall estate became a small island of comparative wealth in a lower-class locality.

If you could afford between £1 000 and £2 000 for your semi-detached house you probably would not choose to live in Bexley at all. Instead, you might look for your home further south, in Chislehurst, or perhaps in Petts Wood, where part of the old woodland was preserved (it is now in the care of the National Trust). The large semi-detached houses there are interspersed with larger, expensive detached houses, and some of the former woodland survives in their extensive gardens. The rural charm of the neighbourhood is fortified by a heavy application of Old English styling, especially in the form of mock timber framing and leaded lights to the windows. You really had arrived if you could afford to live there. You would not have your sights on an Austin, a Ford, Hillman or Morris, for this was Humber, Rover and Wolseley country. You were almost in the stockbroker belt.

When suburban husbands came back from the City on the Southern Electric at the end of the 1930s to their new semi-detached houses and the suppers their wives had cooked, or when their wives leaned out of

One of the smallest pairs of semi-detached houses on the Blendon Hall estate. Unlike the houses on the neighbouring Meyer's estates they have spacious plots with drives and room for garages.

A pair of the more bizarrely modernist semi-detached houses on the Blendon Hall estate.

their windows to catch the first glimpse of their returning husbands just as Morrells' advertisements depicted them, breathing the fresh air of a Kent that was fast vanishing beyond the ever-extending roads and roofs, they could count many substantial gains from the decade. It had elevated them to a position of unprecedented prosperity, and it showed nowhere better than in their houses. Nevertheless, the 1930s had hardly been a golden age. Fascism went from one black triumph to another abroad, and at home mass unemployment added its bitterness to the hardships of the poor.

When war did come, the more sinister aspects of the 1930s eclipsed their achievements. Neville Chamberlain failed to secure an enduring peace, and his earlier endeavours through interventionist municipal action and government building subsidies failed to solve the housing problem. The subsidies helped to bring semi-detached suburbia into being, but this did not help the unemployed nor those on low wages earned in the old heavy industries. Local authorities found it increasingly hard to build houses with the small and fluctuating state aid that had been on offer in the 1920s and could not compete with private building. They had to charge rents that were so close to the lowest mortgage repayments, if not more than them, that many people who could afford to pay rent would instead endeavour to find the down payment and repay a mortgage. Those who could afford neither stayed in their slums.

The slums became the target for fresh clearances in the 1930s before they became the targets for bombs, and many socialist councils set to work replacing them with large blocks of dwellings, as they had done at the turn of the century. Some of their inspiration came from the Continent, especially Vienna, where the socialist council had built numerous huge blocks of workers' housing in the 1920s such as

Karl-Marx-Hof. In England the blocks of dwellings were usually built in the plain, yet attractive Georgian style of so many council houses between the wars. This was the one style that a speculative builder would hardly ever adopt for his estates of semi-detached houses, simply because the last thing he wanted to do was to make them look like council houses. In a curious twist of fashion, when Ronald Wates, the son of one of the founders of the building firm, came to build a luxurious house for himself and his young family in Streatham shortly before the Second World War, he chose this plain Georgian style. Perhaps he did not want his house to be mistaken for any of the immense number of cheap semi-detached houses he had put up all over south London for the new suburbanites.

Young architects who believed in the ideals of the Modern Movement had no patience with this preoccupation with style, what Osbert Lancaster called 'By-pass variegated'. They loathed the mock timbering, they loathed the little boxy rooms, they loathed the endless unplanned sprawl and haphazard layout of semi-detached estates. Possibly they were envious of a success that they had had no part in promoting. Their ideas were anyway quite different. Mass-produced concrete and glass that let the sun flow healthily into wide open living spaces were the answer, and planned blocks of dwellings and high-density housing set in green parkland. That, they believed, could be a Utopia for all, if only they had the chance to build it. The destruction brought by the Second World War gave them that chance. In 1945 the prospect of a bright new future was, for them, truly enchanting: it was goodbye to the cloyingly confined atmosphere of petty individuality that ruled suburbia.

'By-pass variegated' in Bexley: the semi-detached suburban house nevertheless remains as desirable as ever.

So-minded architects and planners did have a point. They firmly believed that semi-detached houses stood for smug self-satisfaction, the less justified because they had been too cheap. If anyone had paid the price for the wasted countryside that became suburbia it was not

semi-detached suburban Mr James, nor the builders who provided for him and made the profits. Perhaps it was the original residents of villages like old Bexley who had been engulfed by the new houses. At all events, the real poor had been unable to share in the new prosperity. A few found cheap lots of land, especially in Essex to the east of London, and built themselves shacks or tiny bungalows, but many of them were left in their slums.

Yet for some two and a half million families – ten million people, at least – the dream of a house of their own had come true. Architects, who were generally excluded from building semi-detached suburbs, are now more circumspect in condemning them for the failings they were so quick to denounce in the 1930s and 1940s. Since 1945 they have often aimed higher but achieved less. Some of what they have built has more obviously and more painfully failed. Some of it is already indistinguishable from the slums they hoped to replace. That is not a charge to be raised against suburbia. People who go to live there now still find it desirable. The houses can be modernised and made comfortable. True, they are a bit boxy, but they do not lack space. They endlessly repeat a formula, but people like this formula and can impress their individuality on it.

Champions of these semi-detached houses have admiringly called them the vernacular architecture of the 1920s and 1930s. That will not do. The term 'vernacular' implies regionalism. These houses are too widespread and too standardised for that; you could never tell the difference between Bexley's semi-detached houses and those of Birmingham. In a way, these houses are more like the spoken English that the BBC was broadcasting when it was new, Standard English South, with a caricatured version of regional accents added for variety when needed. One thing is hard to dispute: never again were we to build so extensively and so indiscriminately, nor were we ever to satisfy so many people so quickly.

CHAPTER EIGHT
Power to the People

Liverpudlians are proud of Toxteth just as they are proud of Everton, Edge Hill, Anfield and Wavertree. They live in the finest city in the north and know it. But outsiders who do not share this fierce attachment to where they live see Liverpool, and especially Toxteth, in a different light. They see deprivation, poverty and blight, everything that is wrong with our inner city areas.

Even as you pass the cathedral on the way out to Toxteth, the blight becomes evident all around. Acres of rubble show where terraces of substandard houses and tenements of stacked dwelling units once housed some of the densest populations in the country. Three hundred people to the acre was quite usual. Many more of these dwellings still stand, covered in graffiti, boarded-up and waiting for the demolition men. Here and there a house or a flat is still occupied. You can tell because the windows are clean and have curtains, not boards across them, nor gaping holes.

You can see this all round Liverpool, and in most of our large cities for that matter, where declining populations and declining wealth have brought fresh problems. If you want a quick glance at it all, take Park Road through Toxteth, but even here the picture is not entirely of devastation in every direction. Many of the tenements and terraces are still occupied. There are plenty of new houses going up too, and there is a bustling market full of busy people. Liverpudlians do not take life

Liverpool tenements – 'piggeries' – built between the wars and now boarded up, defaced by graffiti, yet still occupied by a few families.

lying down. Hard years of declining fortunes may have made them sceptical, but, given the chance, they have the energy to build on Liverpool's best traditions. In fact the City Corporation (Scousers condescend to call it the 'Corpie') is busy building as well as tearing down what it built twenty years ago. The mistakes of the past are being eradicated.

What the Corporation is building is certainly different. The semi-detached houses now rising from the rubble will make the tenement blocks and slabs and towers of the past fifty years look very inhuman indeed. Liverpudlians hate blocks of flats; they call them 'piggeries'. What they want is a recognisable house with a front door and a plot of land.

If this were all they wanted, the mistakes of the past might be on their way to being undone. But people do want more. They want a say in where they are to be housed. They want to stick with their friends, whom they have relied on to help them out of trouble and whom they have supported through years of trial. They do not want to be sent miles from where they used to live. Further, they want a say in running their homes for themselves. That means a lot more than being decanted from a rotting terrace or the concrete wastes of a tottering estate of tower blocks to a neat little brick box with a front door opening on to a patch of garden.

By and large, around the country this has been attained and more. Mostly people have done it by buying their homes, though that has not been the only way. Nearly two-thirds of us now own our homes, compared with eighty years ago when fewer than one in ten did so. To be an owner-occupier is no longer to join an elite; it is normal. That has been the major change in housing this century. It has nothing to do with architecture, but everything to do with politics and economics. Rent controls have reduced the number of private landlords to a shadow of their former numbers, and tax relief on mortgages has been a great incentive to buy. These policies have been maintained by all our political parties. The spread of affluence across an expanding middle class to even better-paid manual workers continued after the Second World War at an unprecedented level, while taxation tended to reduce the gap between the highest and the lowest paid. All this brought about a great demand for small houses to buy, which private building tried hard to supply.

Public building by local authorities also tried to fulfil the needs of those numerous people unable to afford their own houses. Arguably, it provided them with standards of accommodation as measured by government recommendations that were no worse than those provided for owner-occupiers and, in some ways, with standards that were better.

These standards were set by the successors to the 1918 Tudor Walters report – first the Dudley report of 1944 and then the Parker Morris report of 1961. Parker Morris moved away from a rigid insistence on minimum sizes for specific rooms, and instead proposed minimum overall areas related to the number of occupants of a house and the functions of the rooms it should accommodate. Living areas, the report proposed, should be divided into a communal one, where a family could talk, eat and entertain together, and a private area, where they could relax, study or work quietly. This division was like a modern interpretation of the medieval arrangement of hall and chamber, though the new rooms were physically very different and not intended for sleeping in. The parlour was meanwhile forgotten. This sounds like a victory at last for the planners and architects, but in fact it resulted from changes in life-styles. Moreover, houses were now rather larger than the old two-up, two-down houses, and certainly cleaner and better equipped than at the start of the century. There was now no need for a ritual room that was spotless because it was unused during much of the week; a mantelpiece or a shelf or two of photographs and souvenirs were enough for most people.

Parker Morris recommended better heating throughout the house than used to be provided by individual fireplaces. Coal fires had to be replaced by smokeless fuel because of the post-war clean-air Acts, but hot and cold running water and central heating, especially when fired by clean, piped fuels such as oil or gas, saved labour, were easily controlled and more efficient. At the same time efficiency in the kitchen was pursued by recommending larger rooms than the old poky sculleries, and the efficient layout of sinks, cookers and working surfaces. Here the Parker Morris report might have gone further had it anticipated the flood of modern kitchen appliances, the spread of plumbed-in washing-machines and, to a much smaller extent, dishwashers, and the benefits of freezers as well as refrigerators. None the less, it was aware of the general increase in household possessions and so emphasised the need for more storage space than before. Unfortunately, the Parker Morris standards were never more than recommendations. The minimum standards that the report proposed were too often taken as the maximum standards for both private and public housing.

Housing often failed for other reasons than falling below the Parker Morris standards. Because of the chronic post-war housing shortage or because of poverty, many people still had to rent substandard houses or flats in subdivided houses from landlords who either would not maintain them properly or, because of rent controls, sometimes could not afford to maintain them. These houses were often ruled unfit for habitation and declared slum clearance areas. This did not necessarily ensure immediate clearance, but it invariably did put a full stop to any further maintenance. Instead of the speedy rehousing that should then have followed, it easily led to the kind of blight so prevalent in Toxteth, where nobody cared but the tenants; they could not help themselves.

Other more fortunate people were able to go into the public housing that had expanded so greatly after the Second World War. The trouble was that council dwellings might comply with Parker Morris standards but still be unsatisfactory. Because of poor design or shoddy construction – especially factory construction that was intended to be cheap and quick but was actually neither – such dwellings often failed to live up to their specifications. Others were satisfactory in themselves, but were set in the bleakest of surroundings. Still others suffered from lackadaisical maintenance, which was so slow in being carried out that they fell deeper and deeper into disrepair. Tenants found councils unresponsive and bureaucratic. It is easy to see how Liverpool's Corpie got its bad name. It was a case of 'them and us'.

Tenants in such situations were trapped. They were powerless to help themselves. They could seldom afford to buy their way out, and even when their needs were judged important enough to warrant notice, there was always someone in a worse position, and usually whole queues of them. In Liverpool, where the old sources of wealth – docks, shipbuilding, sugar-refining, tobacco – had been declining for a generation, these problems were particularly aggravated by the failing economy. Increasingly, unemployment gnawed at the people, as it still does. The large bonfire that the Toxteth rioters made of derelict houses in July 1981 was an unmistakable signal of distress.

Well before that, another group of local people was completing the first stages in what might become a new revolution in housing. There was no question of waiting for the ashes of Toxteth to cool; they had already started on their path to revitalise the place four years earlier, when in 1977 they formed the Weller Streets Housing Co-operative.

They were enabled to do this because the Housing Corporation, which the government had set up in 1974, was allowed to provide public money for a housing association prepared to build or renovate housing on a non-profit-making basis. A group like the Weller Streets Housing Co-operative was eligible for public funds to do this, even though working-class people had never built houses for themselves in this way before. Members of this co-operative were proud of Toxteth and had their roots there. Though they lived in officially declared slums, they wanted to stay together and this they did. They were not well off, so there was no question of buying their way out, and that, anyway, would have done nothing to help them as a group. They had a strong belief in democratic organisation, despite earlier setbacks when appealing to the Corporation on a local issue. Led by their local milkman, who knew everyone in the Weller Streets area, and by a trade unionist from Fords at Halewood, they found a way of getting new houses for themselves nearby, and came to point the way for other groups to follow.

Their achievement has been hailed as a great success. Royalty has given them its blessing with a visit, and the government has smiled on their initiative. They have won a housing award. There is indeed reason to be proud of Toxteth now. But, there is a note of dissent amid the widespread acclaim. It comes from the City Corporation, and shows how deeply political issues have scarred the question of who should provide the houses.

In order to understand the achievement of the Weller Streets Housing Co-operative and the controversy it has aroused, you must first look at what was built. Turn off Park Road at Byles Street, and on the left you come to blocks of walk-up tenements, so described because of the public staircases that give access to individual flats. The tenements are neither large, nor old, nor grim: in fact, they are not bad for Liverpool. Even so, the buildings on the other side of the road provide a complete contrast. Here is the Weller Streets Housing Co-operative's estate. The members chose to build their new homes in the form of ten L-shaped terraces of red-brick houses, laid out to form a series of interconnecting courts, with an access road running into it. They call the road Weller Way, and if you catch the hint of a punning snub to the Corpie and all officialdom, they will not object. There are sixty-one houses in all, mostly fairly similar, but with six different layouts of rooms. Cobbles, sets and paving define pathways that lead across the courts through shrubberies to the porches of the individual houses. At once they look welcoming and private.

Weller Way, a complete contrast to Liverpool's older housing estates.

One of the Weller Streets families at home in the kitchen/dining room they helped to design.

This is real architecture, and of an especially pleasing kind. More importantly, this is a community. Here people understand how communities live and look after themselves, for that is what they do. They got their houses built by their own initiative. It took them through the whole drawn-out process of forming a housing co-operative, obtaining a grant of £1·6 million, getting permissions, finding and purchasing the land, commissioning the architects and designing their houses, building them and then occupying them. The community spirit they began with was severely tested by this, and several people dropped out or were pushed out for failing to back their involvement with some work, but the spirit came through to the end. The houses they built have allowed it to flourish, but the architecture and the landscape of Weller Way is an expression of this community spirit, not its cause.

To recognise this requires a significant shift of opinion. Architectural design may diminish community spirit or it may act as a catalyst to help it come into being, but it cannot create it. This was not understood by post-war architects and planners, nor by their political masters. Some have not understood it yet.

The official ideology is that those who know best about housing are those who are professionally involved in providing it, not those who live in it. This entrenched belief grew up with the paternalistic, benevolent housing movement in the nineteenth century, and came to be espoused by the housing architects of local authorities like the LCC in the middle of this century. The specialist knew best.

The trouble with this belief was that it was not tested by practice. When the LCC built the world's largest council estate in the wilderness of Becontree to the east of London between 1921 and 1934 and decanted the slum dwellers of the East End out there, it failed to realise the full implications of the disruption, loneliness and sheer desperation it caused, though there was little wrong with the houses it had built.

These problems were compounded because those responsible for housing were easily persuaded by architectural arguments and simply forgot the prospective tenants. As the Weller Streets people have said, architects only saw tenants by accident. Had these architects and the planners and, above all, the housing managers in the local authorities, considered their problem outside its narrowly architectural and bureaucratic context, they might have realised that communities cannot be created by architectural means alone. When at last they did, the method they had created of building public housing was in full swing and hard to stop.

By the 1940s the old Victorian idea that certain styles of architecture had a moral worth that could improve people had given way to a more sophisticated belief that the new blessings of Modern Movement architecture applied to public housing could provide everything that people wanted. The freedom that a reinforced concrete frame gave to a building in theory allowed an architect to make its interior infinitely adaptable because the walls no longer carried the weight of the floors above. As these walls were no longer load-bearing, they could have large windows wherever was most convenient. Good lighting was a concomitant of good health, and came to be almost mystically imbued with some of the moral qualities that had once been associated with the Christian styles of architecture, like Gothic for churches and Old

English for houses. Furthermore, the healthy aspect of a block of dwellings and its moral aspect as well were enhanced by setting it in open parkland so that fresh air could circulate around it as well as light penetrate it. In this way the old, supposedly moral virtues of architecture came to be transferred from styles revived from the past to the new architecture of the twentieth century that was widely believed to transcend mere style altogether.

Building in this way was not by itself enough. Long before the Second World War the arch-exponent of modernism, the Swiss architect Le Corbusier, realised that housing must be supported by shops, social centres and other communal amenities, ideally all accommodated in the same building as the dwelling units. His ideas widely influenced the new generation of English architects practising after the Second World War, even as his own Unité d'Habitation was rising in Marseilles to exemplify his ideals.

The provision of social amenities was not all. The planners appreciated that though standard families with two and a half children might preponderate on their new estates, reality was more complicated. They would have to provide for larger families, for childless couples, for the aged, perhaps for single people. An estate should therefore have a wide range of accommodation, varying in size to cater for these differing groups of occupants. In this way the large mixed development came into being. Much housing provided by local authorities, however, lacked both this variety and a range of social amenities. Local councils were often concerned with building the largest number of dwelling units for their money, not creating the best environments for people.

Today it is recognised that much public housing was not fully attuned to people's day-to-day lives. The resulting buildings were often radically different from those of the past, but there was one common factor that went back to the origins of charitable housing and its underlying support for belief in social improvement. The people who were to live on the new estates had still never been asked for their opinions. There was a wide chasm between those in need – the tenants – and those who had the professional responsibility of providing for them. The planners thought they knew what was best for the tenants, and, like it or not, that is where the tenants were housed.

Many tenants in fact did like it. Often they came from terrible housing conditions and were overjoyed by all that the architects and planners had given them. The trouble came when the novelty wore off. Then people realised that however good their individual dwellings were, the surroundings were badly planned. In the more poorly designed estates, this happened in a matter of days. The buildings too failed to live up to their promise, and increasingly needed more maintenance than the local authorities were prepared to carry out. Some estates soon got so bad a name that they were hard to let. That happened widely in Liverpool, where the number of empty Corporation dwellings rose into thousands. No one would live in them. The amenities provided on the estates were often second-rate if there were any at all, and unable to compete with what was commercially available elsewhere.

The families themselves changed. Some grew as children were born, others contracted as children grew up and left home, or as the

Contrasts in housing in Liverpool: twenty storeys of dwelling units built in the 1960s at Edge Hill loom over five storeys built in the 1930s, and three storeys built in the nineteenth century along Crown Street.

elderly died. A possible solution would have been to move people around into more suitable dwelling units to accommodate these changes, but local authorities were not well prepared for this either. In any case, no one wants to move simply because the family has lost a son or gained a daughter. The flexibility that modern design hinted that it could provide never extended as far as this. Constant moving with every change, had it occurred, would have been as damaging as the overcrowding of some dwelling units and the under-occupation of others. Stable neighbourly relations and a sense of community were never given much consideration. Either the planners thought that people would take it all in their stride aided by the benefits of modern architecture, or they did not think about it all. As for the housing managers, they had as much as they could do struggling with the endless waiting lists and the problems of filling the unsuitable estates presented to them by the architects and planners.

The success of public housing should not be minimised, but signs that it was far from outstanding began to emerge in the middle of the 1960s. As expectations rose with increasing affluence, it became clear that much new housing was unsuitable, especially in multi-storey towers or slabs, and that the standards of construction were often poor. It also became clear that, however fast houses were built, the housing problem stubbornly remained acute in cities like Liverpool.

In the later 1960s national confidence began to waver, affecting society at large as well as housing. People began to question what had been achieved since the Second World War. Where housing itself was concerned, the worries suddenly took on all the semblance of a public crisis in 1968 when a gas explosion ripped the side off Ronan Point, a tower block of flats at Canning Town in east London. Twenty-three storeys of housing units collapsed like a pack of cards, exposing their pitiful rooms and a much vaunted but technically unsound modern construction system at the same time. There was a growing realisation that it was not only the construction of housing estates that was failing. Graffiti covered the walls of onerous stairways, of lifts that were too often out of order, of dank draughty access balconies, and of all the unwelcoming areas of the estates that were neither public enough nor private enough. The whole environment of much public housing was causing anger and despair.

Ordinary people found the cost of the new architectural vision higher than they were willing to pay. You might grumble at the rent, though subsidies, grants, controls and rebates kept what you paid to a level you were supposed to be able to afford. But you also paid in something far less tangible, the network of communal links that had once welded streets of working-class families together. Splitting them up and decanting them to the new estates had broken this spirit, and the fragmented layout of the new dwellings did nothing to build new relationships. It is hard to get on with neighbours you hear overhead but never see next door. The adversity of struggling up several storeys of stairs with shopping, pram and toddlers did nothing to cement relationships, nor did the concrete and glass of the new Utopia.

The one thing that the Weller Streets Housing Co-operative was sure of was its community spirit. Its members lived in rows of streets named after characters in Dickens. Weller Street cut across them and

These were old homes where the Weller Streets families had spun a web of ties, condemned and empty and waiting for demolition.

gave the area its name. It was full of terraces of decayed two-up, two-down houses, built in the 1860s on the smallest scale allowed by the by-laws of those days. They were like the houses of the same period in Preston, but with the advantage of having back lanes, called 'entries' in Liverpool, to provide access to the rear of the houses. Even so, they were too small to modernise and were beyond repair, which was sad since they had seen generations of families born, grow up and die together. These familes had spun a web of ties that were immediately threatened when the houses were designated as a slum-clearance area.

In some ways the threat was worse because it was so ill defined. Reputedly, the area was fifty-seventh on the list for action. Sometime in the distant future, when the Corporation at last got down to it, the houses would be emptied. One by one, the occupants would be decanted to whatever suitable council housing could be found around Liverpool, no one knew where, and perhaps even as far away as the estates in Kirkby and Speke. There each family would have to pick itself up, alone among new faces, and start life afresh. Weller Street and the rest would be obliterated. Meanwhile, the occupiers of this area had to wait while their houses crumbled. After all, no one would do more than immediate repairs to a house scheduled for eventual demolition.

Placidly watching their homes and the whole neighbourhood fall apart was anathema to the group of residents who formed the Weller Streets Housing Co-operative. They were determined to solve their problems for themselves and unwilling to let anything stand in their way, especially establishment officialdom. They could have done no better than heed John Lennon's lines.

> There's nothing you can make, that can't be made,
> No one you can save that can't be saved,
> Nothing you can do, but you can learn how to be you in time.
>   It's easy.
> (*All You Need is Love*, Lennon/McCartney)

Even the maddeningly inverted sense of his words is appropriate to their cause. They had to turn upside down the 'it can't be done' attitude. Luckily they knew differently. It was not easy, despite what the Beatles sang, and they needed persistence, patience, and an indomitable spirit as well as love.

In theory at least, the process of building by a housing co-operative is straightforward. Tenants in officially recognised housing-need organise themselves into a formally registered housing co-operative. To do this, they need the instruction, if not the services of a management agency like Merseyside Improved Houses or Co-operative Development Services, which first explained the system to the Weller Streets group. As soon as the co-operative is formed it must get official recognition in principle so that it can receive public funds through a housing association grant. This is needed to cover the large gap between what the co-operative will be able to afford from the fair rent it charges its members and the total amount it must pay for the construction of its houses. The co-operative must then find a suitable site on which to build. This is most likely to come from a local authority – in the Weller Streets case Liverpool City Corporation or Merseyside Development Corporation. Once the co-operative has found a site, it must choose an architect to design the housing it wants. It then submits its proposed scheme to a funding body, which might be the Housing Corporation or the Liverpool City Corporation. Next, the proposals go to the Department of the Environment for approval, to ensure that they reach the required standards, formerly the Parker Morris standards, now abandoned, and come within the government's imposed financial limits for public housing. When these hurdles have been cleared, building may start. At its conclusion the housing co-operative becomes the collective owner of the estate of completed houses and leases them to the individual member-tenants at a fair rent officially agreed by the local rent officer. The rent pays for the management and maintenance of the estate as well as for repaying the part of the cost of the site and the houses not covered by the grant.

When the Weller Streets people started on this course, they were prompted by desperate determination, a combination of vision and anger, as Alan MacDonald has recounted in *The Weller Way: the Story of the Weller Streets Housing Co-operative*. They met all the difficulties of being the first to find a way through the procedural maze. Compounding these difficulties was the refusal of many officials to believe that they could make their way at all, not to mention downright obstruction. But first of all the co-operative had to persuade its own people that they could win through. Not all were persuaded, and even those who were did not all act as quickly as one who said, 'I liked the idea of setting up a co-op. I thought it was a bit of a fight and I wanted to get involved in it . . . This is going to work y' know.'

It was a fight. Everything they did had to be learned from scratch. A housing co-operative has to learn how to form itself into a committee and run itself with a chairman, secretary and treasurer. The Weller Streets group pooled every ounce of experience they possessed, and aggressively covered over what they lacked until they could learn it. This did not immediately endear them to outsiders. They were their own worst enemies, or so officials thought, because they wanted to do everything for themselves, and took the attitude that professionals were there to serve them, not vice versa. Indeed, they were obstinately

Uniform red bricks and imaginative planting characterise the ten courtyards of Weller Way.

The Leta-Claudia Housing Co-operative's Mere Green, with its access road curving between crescents of houses and round the communal lounge on the right.

Thirlmere Green, terrace houses for families on the left, bungalows for retired people on the right.

sceptical of anyone in authority, and sometimes downright distrustful. This was an attitude they had had all their lives, and their new experiences did nothing to soften their belief that the world was indeed divided into 'them and us'.

These divisions cut many ways. Four hundred families lived in the Weller Streets area, but only seventy-one joined the group although all were given the opportunity. Nevertheless, the local Labour Party called it queue-jumping. The committee members who ran the co-operative always had to keep an eye on all the members, and agonised over the possibility that a feeling of 'them and us' might develop even among themselves, the committee who did the leading and the general members who were led. Everything that was decided had to be *generally* acceptable as well as being the majority's wish, and the committee did its best to ensure that this was so. That approach was all the more difficult to carry through when so many problems were hard to understand and harder to explain. Work is always hard for the committee, but the committe members drove on and did their best to keep the general members behind them. They underplayed failures and delays, but thankfully there was enough progress to keep them all unified.

Finding a site is always a major problem. A co-operative has to do this itself. Toxteth seemed to be full of derelict land, but when investigated it always turned out to be reserved for some nebulous purpose. Land-use and ownership were obstacles apparently set up to keep land unoccupied for ever. At last after eight months came the promise of the Byles Street site, though not before the local Labour councillors had refused to support the co-operative and the Liberals had offered them a smaller site that would have divided the group and made even more of an elite of the lucky few who could have built on it. Getting the site involved a political struggle because the county council had to be made to abandon defunct plans to slap a ring road through it, but in the end this had the advantage of bringing back the support for the scheme of the political parties on the Corporation.

Housing co-operatives, however enthusiastic, always need professional help. From the start, the Weller Streets Co-operative had the

'*Here we go*'. *A group photograph taken after a successful site meeting of the Hesketh Street Housing Co-operative.*

help of Co-operative Development Services. This was indispensable, but relations were never close between the two. The agency wanted to decide too much, and the fees they charged were another source of friction. In the end the ferociously independent spirit of the Weller Streets committee shattered the increasingly embittered relationship.

Suspicion built up during the process of choosing a firm of architects and then obtaining a design. The Weller Streets people wanted to design their houses for themselves without intermediaries. They found that they could *actually do so*, at least in part. One of their members had worked in the building industry and could not only put this experience at the group's disposal, but also had the great advantage of having a three-dimensional understanding of architectural drawings. The co-operative was lucky in finally finding so sympathetic an architect in Bill Halsall who worked for Building Design Group, now called Wilkinson Hindle and Partners. In this way they usurped much of Co-operative Development Services' responsibilities, and that increased tension. Nevertheless, it sharpened the Co-operative's resolve. The Co-operative formed into two design committees, one for the inside and the other for the outside of the proposed dwellings, though of course they had to come together once some of the basic ideas had been settled. Bill Halsall had to act as their teacher as well as their designer, because they were determined to tell him what they wanted, rather than he tell them what he thought they should have. That was their attitude to everything, but Halsall admired them and they accepted him. 'It's like teaching the first three years of an architecture course to seventy people in six weeks', he said, 'but it's a mutual process.' It was an unusual process too, with a very different kind of rigour from that which you would find in an ordinary architectural training. Many professional pre-conceptions had to be forgotten.

It began well. Most co-operatives go to see other local housing schemes, and the Weller Streets group got their first ideas this way too. Then discussions round a table led to the two design committees sketching out their ideas, and these were drawn up by Halsall and revised until they achieved a general consensus of approval. Giving them what they wanted was what guided Halsall, whose job was, as he saw it, to turn their ideas into architecture. It was not simply a matter of him doing what he was told, and if anything it increased his responsibilities to them.

'Uniformity versus diversity was an argument that was a sticking point with a lot of people,' Halsall remembers. Resolving this issue has to be faced by all co-operatives, but for the Weller Streets group it led to a philosophical discussion that touched on their very nature. As far as possible equality was to be the rule, and this led to two important decisions, both designed to ease management. The first was to restrict the number of house plans to six and to standardize fittings and other details. This simplified design and for the future would also simplify the allocation of houses both in the first instance and when second-generation members came to join the co-operative. The members agreed, from political conviction and aesthetic consideration as well as from this practical need for simplicity, that all the members must accept majority decisions on standardised details, whether they were door fittings or even white enamelled baths. While equality was one

Planning the ten courts. The Weller Streets group considered several possible layouts using Bill Halsall's models to guide them before the final layout was adopted.

rule, quality was another, so far as they could afford it, but green baths for those who wanted them and would pay the extra cost were ruled out. So were individually chosen door knockers.

The second choice that was made was to divide the estate into ten courts. The idea of having courtyards came from a visit to the Ribblers Lane estate in Liverpool, which they much liked, though the layout greatly changed as their design proceeded. It had advantages for management since they could form into sub-groups, court by court, that would have some autonomy. Interestingly, while they agreed that each sub-group could choose the colour of the bricks to differentiate the courts, they all individually chose red and in the end built all the courts of houses in the same red.

The courtyard plan raised objections from the City Engineer, and the co-operative had to fight hard to have them. One stipulation he raised was that each courtyard had to have a roadway with a large hammerhead layout to enable articulated lorries to turn round. Those were the rules. But this would have destroyed the layout, and anyway it was also opposed in principle. 'The whole point was that we didn't want articulated lorries turning in our courtyards,' explained one member. They eventually won the day, but the City Engineer refused to allow the Corporation to adopt the roadways within the courts, so they remain the co-operative's responsibility to this day. Later they retaliated by insisting on calling the access road 'Weller Way'. The

One of the ten courts built by the Weller Streets Housing Co-operative with flats for the elderly set into the angle between the ranges of houses.

*'A little bit of heaven': new homes
for the Weller Streets families
and a party to celebrate.*

Corpie thought that 'Weller Close' would be nicer. Perhaps it would, but the Weller Streets people did not achieve success by being nice to those in authority.

All this took place between 1977 and October 1982 when the last of the Weller Streets families moved in to the new estate. They had not been sunk by bureaucracy during those five wearying years, nor by the furiously assertive way in which they had attained their dream. Now they have to live with this dream and resolve the new problems of getting on together without the unifying factor of the original fight. In place of that fight, they have the unifying factor of what they fought for – their homes. 'We didn't realise we were coming to a Utopia,' one said: and another, 'It's a little bit of heaven, this.'

There are now thirty-seven housing co-operatives in Liverpool. Since the Weller Streets Co-operative was formed, most of them have followed suit and built their own houses, rather than just renovating older ones. Some co-operatives are fully self-managing like Weller Streets, others employ agents for some services. Hesketh Street Housing Co-operative, for example, employs Co-operative Development Services to provide maintenance and financial services. Leta-Claudia and Thirlmere Housing Co-operatives both employed Merseyside Improved Houses as a developing agent, but since completion have managed their own affairs. Management is certainly crucial if the co-operatives are to succeed. At present, while success sustains enthusiasm and all the members have the experience of building what they wanted to inspire them, no problems seem insuperable. Even so, the co-operatives will always need members with a capacity for leadership. In twenty years' time when most of the original members will have gone, the real test will come. If they can bequeath their commitment to their successors – and the joy of living in these estates makes that likely even though the unique opportunity of actually creating them will have passed – the future should present no unresolvable problems. If the co-operatives can succeed in those conditions, they will have achieved something denied to council tenants.

Within the framework of the financial restraints imposed by housing grants and the standards set by Parker Morris the residents of these co-operatives were able to chose what they wanted. This depended on the size of each family, but was also a matter of choosing the arrangement of living spaces. Living rooms, dining rooms and kitchens could be kept separate or put together in a variety of combinations. For instance, some people wanted modern, open-plan spaces, while others prefered traditional separate rooms. Similarly, circulation space from the front entrance to the staircase and a back door could be kept separate or open into one or other of the rooms. Smaller details, like the amount and position of storage space, was again for the residents to choose. The combinations are not endless, though the co-operatives and their architects have shown much ingenuity in ringing the changes. The houses are not perfect, as both architects and residents admit. There are all sorts of details they would change now that they have experience of what they have designed, but these are of little consequence compared with the deep satisfaction of having produced their designs through co-operative involvement, and managing the estates themselves afterwards. These houses are real homes.

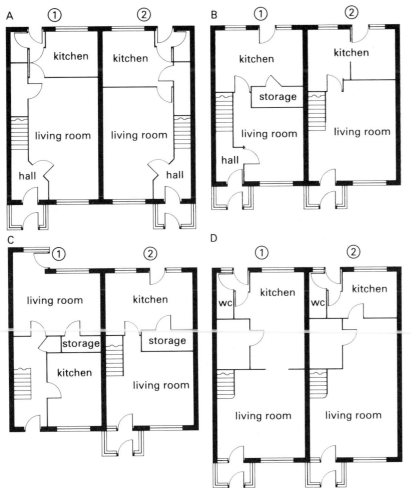

Some variations of plans for the Hesketh Street Housing Co-operative. A, B and C all have three bedrooms, D have four. Some people have chosen open plans without halls and without full partitions between kitchens and living rooms, others have separated the rooms and rung the changes with the amount and position of storage.

Externally, the houses all have the appearance of traditional homes. A little variety expresses their individuality. They are all of brick, but, despite being factory made, these display a great variety of types and colours throughout the estates. The same goes for the tiles and slates used on the pitched roofs. What is really impressive, however, is not so much the design of the individual houses as the way in which they are laid out. Each estate has a site with its own special characteristics, and each time the residents and architects have responded in a different way. Nevertheless, the estates all achieve a sense of identity and enclosure through their layouts. There are no dead spaces waiting for the vandal with a spray-can.

Instead of the ten small, interlocked courts of Weller Way, for example, the Hesketh Street Co-operative's Newland Court has a large, irregular square where vehicles can turn. It is not littered with amorphous car-parking spaces, but cleverly defined by different sorts of paving and by remarkably lavish garden walls. The irregular form of the square is largely determined by the stepped shape of the site and the way the houses face inwards. Thirlmere Green, which has a similar site to that of Weller Way – rectangular and on a gentle slope – has a large, open square lined with terraces facing inwards on to the access road and an adventure playground under the watchful eye of all the

Extensive planting and an exciting use of walls and entrance piers give Newland Court a remarkable feeling of enclosure.

Variations in the approach to houses.
From left to right: Thirlmere Green windows; Prince Albert Gardens, entrance and access road; Weller Way, path and porches.

The Leta-Claudia group choosing curtain material for their communal lounge.

family houses. At the bottom of the square is a group of bungalows for retired people and, overlooking them, just outside the square, a small block of flats for single people.

Thirlmere Green is at Everton in north Liverpool. A little further out at Walton, just beyond Goodison Park, the Everton football ground, is the Leta-Claudia Housing Co-operative's Mere Green. Nearby, a fragment of the terraces of two-up, two-down houses still remains where some of the residents were born and most lived, though those who had been there only thirty years count themselves newcomers. The site of Mere Green is again rectangular and once had about 150 houses on it divided into terraces fronting Leta and Claudia Streets. Mere Green now has only forty houses, but instead of being arranged as a square, they form a series of inward-facing crescents flanking a sinuous access road that terminates in a tight loop. This surrounds a communal lounge that serves the bungalows at this end. The ingenious layout allows the estate to open up as you pass down it like a series of views that then close behind you.

Prince Albert Gardens is a less contrived version of the same idea. Instead of being flat, the site slopes steeply downhill on the fringes of the city centre, and has spectacular views of the cathedral on the hill above. Here the curving access road is lined by nineteen houses, most of them semi-detached and angled to the axis of the road. This layout once again produces a strong sense of enclosure. Uniquely here, there is a special feeling of belonging to Liverpool, owing to the cathedral looming up the hill. The most remarkable thing about Prince Albert Gardens is not just that the residents all came from a single walk-up tenement, but that most of them are related to one another. The extended family under one roof is rare in England, but here under nineteen roofs you have it. Most of the tenants are middle aged, though there are two households of young single people and an elderly couple. There are only five children. So, although ten houses are designed for families and have three bedrooms each, seven houses have only two bedrooms and two more are in the form of single-bedroom flats.

This arrangement is not an exact reflection of a national trend in society, but serves to illustrate changes in society that housing has increasingly had to accommodate. Historically, marriage, the family and the household have been interdependent. Now marriage and the family are no longer so dominant in society as they once were. Marriage is not the revered institution it was even fifty years ago, divorce is common and so is the establishment of families outside marriage. By contrast, a desire for independence and greater affluence have caused many young people to set up house on their own.

Another social change has been brought about by advances in medicine which have raised life expectancy and extended widowhood. Consequently, households not based on families have doubled to over a quarter of the total in only twenty years, and most of these house single people. Meanwhile, households of married couples with children have declined from about a half to little over a third, and single-parent families account for a tenth of all households.

The layouts of some of the Liverpool housing co-operatives estates showing the great variety of enclosures achieved by the different blocks of houses.

Weller Streets

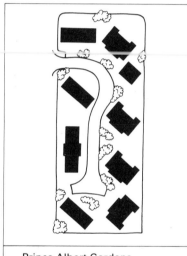

Prince Albert Gardens

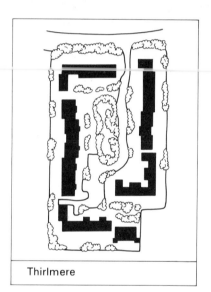

Thirlmere

Hesketh Street

Leta-Claudia

Southern Crescent

Prince Albert Gardens does not, of course, cater for so exact a cross-section of households as these, nor do the housing co-operatives generally. Even so, many of them reflect the new needs, like those of the aged and those living alone. Some of the earlier co-operatives, whose aim was rehabilitation and conversion, not new building, successfully provided bed-sitters for single people. Most radically, Princes Park Co-operative has built a hostel with twenty-three bedrooms for mothers and children who have been forced out of their homes by domestic violence, and Liverpool Gingerbread Housing Co-operative is providing groups of rehabilitated houses for lone parents.

Other co-operatives provide for a wide range of minority groups. Huyton Community Co-operative is building especially for the elderly, but a more interesting provision for them socially is how they have been accommodated by the unspecialised housing co-operatives. Thirlmere Green has bungalows for its elderly inhabitants, and Mere Green provides a communal lounge as well. The approach of Weller Way is to integrate flats for the elderly into their terraces, placing them for maximum security in the angles of the L-shaped blocks and providing them with an alarm system. This gives architectural recognition to the fact that the elderly have special needs, but without ostracising them or even separating them in any way from the community as a whole. In this way architectural form and a specific and positive attitude to social values as determined by the residents themselves have come together in a wholly admirable way – significantly, without anything to do with architectural style.

Under the watchful eye of the family houses, the retired occupants of the Thirlmere Green bungalows have devoted their sunny, sheltered corner to flourishing gardens.

Nevertheless, architectural style must not be forgotten. It may not be directly capable of promoting health as was once thought, but it is able to give pleasure and contribute to happiness. To say the least, all these co-operative housing estates are attractive and have genuine architectural merit. Some are thoroughly successful – the first, Weller Way, being truly outstanding. This is remarkable, given the initial suspicion of the members towards the architects Wilkinson Hindle and Partners and their determination to make all the decisions about design. There is an overlying simplicity about the scheme, which relies for its effect on the proportions of the parts and their placing, from the individual windows through to the overall arrangement and massing of the terraces themselves. Their Housing Centre Trust Jubilee Award was well earned. Mere Green at Walton and Southern Crescent back in Toxteth, by the same architects, have some of these qualities too. Newland Court by Innes Wilkin Ainsley Gommon, and Thirlmere Green by Merseyside Improved Houses Urban Services, both winners of commendations, rely for their effect more on fine detailing and decoration than on proportion and overall form.

Much of the success of the design of the Weller Way houses lies in the careful proportioning and alignment of windows and doors.

In a wider context, the architectural style of these estates reflects the properly homely but not particularly adventurous fashion current among house builders today. Some of the ideas employed at Weller Way can be seen at Ribblers Lane and Runcorn New Town, which the residents visited when they were looking for inspiration before the design process began, and Newland Court similarly takes its cue from Warrington New Town.

None of this in fact matters. The main thing that the Liverpool housing co-operatives are unanimous about is that their houses should not resemble those that the Corporation builds. It is not just because of the special effort that has gone into designing their houses, but because they detest the Corporation's style. As the chairman of one co-operative said,

> It's boring, pathetic, inhuman – like someone went into the architect's department and said, 'I want four hundred houses – get the drawings in by half-three.' They're not houses for people.

Yet there is no strong reason why the architecture of a housing co-operative should be widely different from the architecture of a housing authority or of a speculative builder, or even that it should be outstanding or radically new at all. The planning of the rooms needs to work well, and the layout and the design of the houses needs a sense of identity. That is the main thing. The vernacular architecture of our yeoman forefathers was seldom more than that. It was stylish for its day, but not particularly up to date. It was what people wanted, within the limits of their purses and what was locally available. A return to this ability to command what you want within similar limits is the truly radical achievement started by the Weller Streets Housing Co-operative. It is all the more radical given that they were able to grasp enough power to change their circumstances, though they started with no power at all.

Weller Streets sees it as an expression of 'power to the people', rather than a mere compromise between the benefits of home ownership and the communal responsibility of state ownership. There is no

A kitchen at Newlands Court, designed for the most efficient use of space. It is one of a number of variations, of which some incorporate an eating area.

doubt that they are right, because they have re-established the direct link between the provider and the user. There is only one further stage that this radical method could achieve, and that would be for the individual members of the co-operative to build the houses physically themselves, as is happening on one or two small estates in south London. But that would be to deny themselves the skills and craftsmanship that are essential in the construction of their houses. To be radical you do not always have to resort to first principles, nor to learn all the various building crafts as well.

Far more to the point than the argument about whether the housing co-operatives are involved in a compromise or a radical solution to the housing question is whether their contribution has a wider significance and can play any role at all in solving the chronic problem of housing failure and shortage in inner cities.

It is first of all important to recognise that there are many difficulties with housing co-operatives. Not just any group of people is likely to have the determination to take the process of building for themselves to its conclusion. The Weller Streets group, or at least its leaders, were by no means ordinary people. Being first, their task was the harder; so perhaps less determined people may now more easily be able to follow the path they established. But whether many can do this is not yet clear. There is no escaping the fact that only sixty-one families out of the 400 in the Weller Streets area decided to build for themselves. Again, in eight years the Liverpool housing co-operatives have built or planned to build themselves only about 650 new houses for some 2500 people. That is a drop in the ocean compared with a currently estimated housing need in Liverpool of possibly twenty times that amount. The earlier co-operatives like Weller Streets took five years from formation to the occupation of their houses. That is hardly quick, though no slower than most similar schemes, and the delays were not of their own making. The later co-operatives have reduced the time to four years.

The design process, especially the long period of gestation with numerous evenings of consultation between the architects and the members of the co-operatives, puts a strain on local professional resources all to produce houses that do not look significantly different architecturally from thousands of both council houses and privately owned houses all round the country. There is no reason, though, why these resources should not expand and become more efficient to meet a rising demand.

The self-build co-operatives do seem to be an encouraging signpost to a better life even though the method of building is not yet much beyond the prototype stage. It would be a great pity if the Liverpool housing co-operatives went the way of the self-governing Chartist settlements of the 1840s. Their ideals of self-help and freedom from the landlord and the mill owner were in the best tradition of British radicalism, yet their houses, like those at Charterville at Minster Lovell near Witney in Oxfordshire, are no more than a historical curiosity now. The Liverpool co-operatives have far more than the Chartists' indifferent support and should expect a longer and better future. Their estates ought to last far longer than most recent council housing, if only because they are objects of great affection and will be tended lovingly. Yet, if they are to succeed in resolving some of the problems of housing the needy in inner cities, they will have to overcome opposition and build far more houses both quickly and decisively.

The opposition in Liverpool came from the Labour Corporation that was elected in 1983. They see co-operatives as a waste of an immense amount of effort to achieve nothing architecturally very unusual. To them, co-operatives are groups of people, who were admittedly in recognised and acute need of housing, who raised themselves into an elite through exploiting the system of housing grants, jumping to the head of the housing queues, and wasting a lot of time, effort and money to obtain individual housing of a not particularly special kind. They decided that it would have to stop, and took measures to ensure that it did by calling a halt to the system of housing grants that sustained it.

Instead the Corporation prefers to build large numbers of similar houses as quickly as possible to reduce the acute shortage. The Corporation had some justification for doing this. Its Liberal predecessors, who had supported the co-operatives, grossly neglected other housing in Liverpool. But the new Corporation went further. Despite the working-class credentials of the housing co-operatives, and despite the very co-operative nature of their ventures, they saw the Weller Streets group and their followers as the thin end of a wedge driven into socialist solidarity. They felt the co-operatives had been politically exploited by the former Liberal Corporation and its capitalist Conservative supporters. The Liverpool District Labour Party that controls the City Corporation in 1985 claimed, for instance, that the allocation of housing, reduced to the basic question of who should decide who lives next door to you, should never be removed from the control of the local housing authority in a socialist state. To allow choice by leaving it to the collective members of a housing co-operative 'has never been healthy and has usually been reactionary'. Put bluntly, 'You can't control what you don't own'. In a way this is the nub of the matter. House owners and housing co-operative owner-tenants fully appreciate the point. They do not seek political power, but only the control of their own homes. This way they can manage them well and give their lives a fundamental stability. And they thrive on it.

Nevertheless, some people do not like the close community spirit of the Weller Streets people. Those who lack this spirit, as well as the less determined, will always need council housing. For them the question of jumping to the head of housing waiting lists is a sore point. As it happened, the Weller Streets people could have been more quickly housed by the Corporation than by themselves, but the criticism remains. Competing for scarce resources makes it all the harder to reduce the worst aspects of poor housing. Whatever else the co-operatives did in this field, they have not been significantly more economical in their use of resources than builders of houses by other means. The mass of houses now being built by the Liverpool Corporation may be cheaper, and will probably make significant inroads into Liverpool's present housing shortage. The trouble is that the policy has all the semblance of the concentration on numbers that characterised the 1960s and produced as many fresh problems as it solved.

Viewed historically we are today generally better housed than we have ever been. Given the wealth of the country it would be a scandal if this were not so. In the seventeenth century half the population were believed to increase the nation's wealth and were probably well housed into the bargain. The rest, who decreased the nation's wealth, were left to cope as best they could. That double standard thankfully no longer applies. Nevertheless there are still double standards of other kinds. There is the unfortunate opposition – 'them and us' – between owner-occupied and public housing, though architecturally there is now little to distinguish the two. The housing co-operatives have done well to blur this opposition. Even so, they win applause less for this than because they show initiative. Unfortunately, there are still many people whose personal circumstances put them at so great a disadvantage that they are unable to maintain such initiative day by day, let alone month

House and home.

by month, to enable them to solve their own problems. But they have just as much right to good standards of housing integrated into the wider community as anyone else.

The number of those in need of a proper standard of housing is on the increase, while the present parlous state of the economy has brought the building of council houses nearly to a standstill. Public housing is the only kind of housing that can ever be immediately made available to a large number of poor people at a price they can afford, but the only people at present being rehoused are those suffering the worst deprivations and whose needs have reached levels of dire emergency. The remainder must wait and wait.

Money is by no means the only issue, though it is an important one. What housing services there are should be delivered as of right rather than with the authoritarian paternalism that stems from the political zeal of parties of all shades. There should also be changes in the way in which services are provided. Council employees are too often alienated from the people they are serving, and there is no personal accountability if that service fails.

It is not only more housing that is needed, but more tenant participation in its maintenance. With more housing associations and building co-operatives like Weller Streets, and more of the host of other new means of providing homes, as well as more caring public housing, perhaps the age-old willing acceptance of the disadvantaged 'them' and the comfortable 'us' might be overturned. Rather than there being a privileged elite, however large, everyone in all kinds of houses might instead be able to hold themselves and their homes in full esteem.

Chronology of Events

In the following list national events, in particular those relevant to housing in England, are set against the dates of buildings and types of building specifically mentioned in the text.

627		Royal hall of Ad Gefrin in use
1066	Norman Conquest	
c1200		Earliest surviving timber-framed buildings
c1280		Purton Green Farm built
c1300		Cruck halls built at Harwell and Steventon
c1315		Terrace houses built at Goodramgate, York
1348–50	Black Death: first eruption of bubonic plague	
1380s	Chaucer's *Canterbury Tales*	
1381	Peasants' Revolt	
1394–1402		Westminster Hall rebuilt
c1405		First part of Bayleaf Farm built
c1500		First chimney-stacks in vernacular houses
		Paycocke's, Coggeshall, built
1509	Accession of Henry VIII	
c1510		Bayleaf Farm completed
1530s		Last of thousands of hall-houses built in Kent
1550s		Houses with chimney-stacks built at Bloxham
1558	Accession of Elizabeth I	
1577	William Harrison's *Description of England*	
1580	Royal Proclamation forbidding building around London	
1597	Elizabethan Poor Law codifies earlier arrangements for dealing with the poor	
1600s		Houses built with chimney-stacks at Yetminster

1603	Accession of James I	
1630s		Earl of Bedford employs Inigo Jones in development of Covent Garden
1640–49	Civil War and execution of Charles I	
1648		Henry Shaw builds earliest surviving stone house at Saddleworth
1658		Earliest surviving terrace of brick houses in London built at Newington Green
1660	Restoration of Charles II	
1665	Last outbreak of bubonic plague	Inventory of Thomas Downton of Yetminster
1666	Great Fire of London	
1667	Act for Rebuilding City of London	
1680s		Nicholas Barbon building terraces in London
1690	Gregory King's *Scheme . . . of the several families of England*	
1696	Window tax initiated	

1707	Building Act for preventing fire	
1709	Further Building Act for preventing fire	
1714	Accession of George I	
1720s	Defoe's *Tour thro' . . . Great Britain*	
1728		Gibbs's *Book of architecture*
1733	John Kay patents fly-shuttle	
1742		Edmund Buckley rebuilds house at New Tame
1750s		Buckleys build weaving loft at Pinfold Farm
1759		Chambers's *Treatise of civil architecture*
1761		Marylebone New Road encourages development of Islington
1766		Cloth Hall built at Huddersfield
1769		The Coade Artificial Stone Manufactory opens
c1770	Richard Arkwright's spinning jenny	
1773		The Adams' *Works in architecture*
1774	Building Act for preventing fire and jerry-building	
1777	Cotton spinning starts in Preston	

1780s	Start of Industrial Revolution	
1782	First steam-powered cotton mills	
1782		Shore Mill built at Delph
1793	Start of French Wars	
1795		Further weaving loft built at Pinfold Farm
1810		Final expansion of Pinfold Farm
1811		Blaise Hamlet begun
1811–12	Luddite Riots	
1815	French Wars end at Waterloo Economic stagnation	
1820		First back-to-backs built in Saddleworth for workers of Greenfield Mill
1820s		Ashworth builds model estate at Turton
1830s	Chadwick promotes health reform	
1832	First outbreak of cholera	
1837	Accession of Queen Victoria	
1840	Committee on Health of Towns	
1842		Ackroyd starts model estate at Copley
1848	Public Health Act	
1850	Preston Council takes on duties of Local Board of Health	
1851	Window tax repealed	
1855	London's Metropolitan Board of Works formed	
1856		Tomlinsons start to develop Plungington estate in Preston
1858	Local Government Act gives town councils power to make by-laws	
1862–4	American Civil War causes cotton famine in Lancashire	
1865	London's main drainage inaugurated	
1872	Gladstone's Public Health Act	
1874	Preston Council appoints part-time Medical Officer of Health	
1875		First garden suburb started at Bedford Park
1876	Preston's enfeebled by-laws passed	
1879		Slum clearance around Drury Lane
1880	New by-laws make back lanes compulsory in Preston	
1889	London County Council formed	
1890	Housing Act authorises local authority house building	